Hardy
2012

The School Leader's Guide to
Professional Learning Communities at Work™

RICHARD DUFOUR

REBECCA DUFOUR

A Joint Publication

Solution Tree · naesp™

555 North Morton Street
Bloomington, IN 47404
800.733.6786 (toll free) / 812.336.7700
FAX: 812.336.7790

email: info@solution-tree.com
solution-tree.com

Visit **go.solution-tree.com/plcbooks** to download materials related to this book.

Printed in the United States of America

16 15 14 13 12   1 2 3 4 5

Library of Congress Cataloging-in-Publication Data

DuFour, Richard, 1947-
  Essentials for principals : the school leader's guide to professional learning communities at work / Richard DuFour, Rebecca DuFour.
      p. cm.
  Includes bibliographical references and index.
  ISBN 978-1-935543-36-7 (perfect bound : alk. paper) -- ISBN 978-1-935543-37-4 (library edition : alk. paper) 1. Professional learning communities. 2. School management and organization. 3. School principals--Professional relationships. I. DuFour, Rebecca Burnette. II. Title.
  LB1731.D75 2012
  370.71'1--dc23
                        2011044821

Solution Tree
Jeffrey C. Jones, CEO
Edmund M. Ackerman, President

Solution Tree Press
President: Douglas M. Rife
Publisher: Robert D. Clouse
Vice President of Production: Gretchen Knapp
Managing Production Editor: Caroline Wise
Senior Production Editor: Suzanne Kraszewski
Copy Editor: Sarah Payne-Mills
Proofreader: Elisabeth Abrams
Text Designer: Jenn Taylor
Cover Designer: Amy Shock

ACKNOWLEDGMENTS

The premise of this book is that the most effective principals define their role as leaders of a professional learning community. This is certainly not a new concept. In fact, the National Association of Elementary School Principals has urged principals to be leaders of learning communities since 2001. NAESP has sponsored this Essentials for Principals series to provide principals both with an understanding of the challenges inherent in this task, and with the knowledge and skills to succeed in meeting those challenges. We are grateful for the leadership of NAESP and its executive director, Gail Connelly, in the ongoing effort to provide principals with the support they need to be effective in this vitally important position.

We also acknowledge the tremendous support we have received for this project from the Solution Tree family. We could not ask for a more ardent or effective proponent of our work than Jeff Jones, chief executive officer of Solution Tree. Douglas Rife, president of Solution Tree Press, and Gretchen Knapp, vice president of production, were instrumental in bringing the concept of the series to life. Once again, we relied on the skillful editing of Sue Kraszewski to make our ideas more clear and our prose more readable. It is difficult for us to imagine writing a book without her support and guidance. We also remain indebted to Shannon Ritz, the director of professional development for Solution Tree, who has been our envoy and ally for the past ten years.

We have benefitted from the insights and friendship of some of North America's leading educational experts—Bob Marzano, Michael Fullan, Larry Lezotte, Rick Stiggins, Doug Reeves, Dennis Sparks, Tom Sergiovanni, and Jonathon Saphier. No one, however, has been more influential in our thinking than our long-standing colleague, coauthor, and friend, Robert Eaker.

Finally, we acknowledge the educators who have joined forces to demonstrate that "learning for all" can be a collective commitment rather than a catch phrase. Some of our deepest learning has been the result of working with and observing extraordinary principals. We are confident in presenting the recommendations in this book because, thanks to these practitioners, we have witnessed the power of these concepts and practices in the real world of schools.

Solution Tree Press would like to thank the following reviewers:

Michael D. Bayewitz
Principal
Broad Acres Elementary School
Silver Spring, Maryland

Brian Gardner
Principal
A. B. Chandler Elementary School
Corydon, Kentucky

Barbara Klocko
Assistant Professor, Department of
Educational Leadership
Central Michigan University
Mount Pleasant, Michigan

Laurie Little
Principal
Desert Harbor Elementary School
Peoria, Arizona

Sara Matis
Principal
Westside Elementary School
Springville, Utah

Greg O'Connell
Principal
Coolidge Elementary School
Cedar Rapids, Iowa

Bo Ryan
Principal
Woodside Intermediate School
Cromwell, Connecticut

Mark Supa
Principal
Roosevelt Elementary School
Wauwatosa, Wisconsin

Renee Truncale
Principal
Cox Elementary School
Sachse, Texas

Dwayne Young
Principal
Centreville Elementary School
Centreville, Virginia

TABLE OF CONTENTS

Reproducible pages are in italics
Visit **go.solution-tree.com/plcbooks** to download materials related to this book.

Reproducibles

Visit **go.solution-tree.com/plcbooks** to download the following materials related to this book.

Introduction

Why Is Principal Leadership So Important?

Chapter 1

A Data Picture of Our School

Finding Common Ground in Education Reform

Cultural Shifts in a Professional Learning Community

Why Should We Describe the School or District We Are Trying to Create?

Schaumburg School District 54 Mission and Goals

Why Should We Articulate Collective Commitments?

The Professional Learning Communities at Work™ Continuum: Laying the Foundation

Where Do We Go From Here? Worksheet: Laying the Foundation of a PLC

The Professional Learning Communities at Work™ Continuum: Responding to Conflict

Where Do We Go From Here? Worksheet: Effective Communication (Chapter 9)

ABOUT THE AUTHORS

Richard DuFour, EdD, was a public school educator for thirty-four years, serving as a teacher, principal, and superintendent. He is the only educator in Illinois to receive the state's Distinguished Educator Award as a principal and Award of Excellence as a superintendent. He was presented the Distinguished Scholar Practitioner Award from the University of Illinois and the Distinguished Service Award from Learning Forward (previously National Staff Development Council). Dr. DuFour is the author of twenty books and videos and over ninety professional articles. He is one of the nation's leading authorities on implementation of the professional learning community process and consults with school districts, state departments, and professional organizations throughout the world on school improvement strategies.

Rebecca DuFour, MEd, has served as a teacher, school administrator, and central office coordinator. As a former elementary principal, Becky helped her school earn state and national recognition as a model professional learning community. She is one of the featured principals in the *Video Journal of Education* program "Leadership in an Age of Standards and High Stakes." She is also the lead consultant and featured principal for the *Video Journal of Education* program "Elementary Principals as Leaders of Learning." Becky is coauthor of many books and video series on the topic of PLCs. Becky is the recipient of the Distinguished Alumni Award of Lynchburg College. She consults with and works for professional organizations, school districts, universities, and state departments of education throughout North America.

To book Richard DuFour or Rebecca DuFour for professional development, contact pd@solution-tree.com.

INTRODUCTION

The *Essentials for Principals* series offers a rich resource for both aspiring and experienced principals. Each book in the series addresses a topic of vital interest to principals and offers specific steps to help them apply the most-promising strategies in that area to their schools. Ultimately, however, the impact of the insights and recommendations the series will provide will be determined to a large extent by the way in which the principal defines his or her role and the purpose of the school.

What Is the Role of the Principal?

What is the role of the principal? Do not take that question lightly! How you answer it will influence not only how you approach the position but also will significantly impact your effectiveness in meeting its challenges. Do not assume that there is universal agreement regarding the role of the principal. Are principals middle managers who serve as a conduit between the central office and the school's staff to ensure policies others create are implemented efficiently? Or are principals leaders who rally stakeholders around a shared vision of a great school?

If you profess your belief in the idea of the principal as a leader, what kind of leadership is required of a principal? Different researchers have argued that a principal must serve as an instructional leader, transformational leader, servant leader, strategic leader, learning leader, empowering leader, participatory leader, delegatory leader, or moral leader (Fullan, 2011b; Leithwood, Louis, Anderson, & Wahlstrom, 2004; Robinson et al., 2010).

Do not assume there is general agreement on the fundamental purpose of schooling. While mission statements are almost certain to assert the school's purpose is to ensure all students learn, traditionally, schools have not operated that way. You will encounter staff and community members who argue that learning is a function of ability, and thus the school should focus on sorting and selecting students into different tracks based on their innate abilities. Others will argue the school's purpose is merely to provide students with the opportunity to learn rather than to ensure that learning actually takes place. Still others will debate what is worthy of learning and will call for more or less emphasis on specific subject areas or will place higher or lower value on academic outcomes versus affective outcomes. Some will assert that the school should be responsible and accountable for doing *whatever it takes* to ensure high levels of learning for *all* students.

Do not assume that there is consensus on the primary clients you are to serve as principal. The board and superintendent will expect you to be their instrument for the implementation of policy, and to a great extent, your tenure in the position will depend on their perception of your commitment to and effectiveness in serving this purpose. Community members will remind you that their taxes pay your salary and that the school exists to serve the community. Faculty members will argue that the school will be effective only to the extent that you meet their needs—providing them with resources, supporting their decisions, and buffering them from outside interference. It is easy to say that a school exists to meet the needs of its students, but it is sometimes difficult to be a student-centered school when so many different adults demand that the principal do their bidding.

The Underlying Assumptions of This Book

This book is based on four assumptions:

1. The school's primary purpose is to ensure high levels of learning for all students.

2. The most promising strategy for fulfilling that purpose is to develop the staff's capacity to function as a professional learning community (PLC).

3. The principal's role is to lead a collective effort to create a PLC that ensures high levels of learning for students through recursive processes that promote adult learning.

4. Principals play a vital role in creating the conditions that lead to improved learning for both students and the adults in their schools.

The idea that principals should serve as leaders of a learning community is not new. In 2001, the National Association of Elementary School Principals articulated the professional standards for principals in its publication *Leading Learning Communities: Standards for What Principals Should Know and Be Able to Do.* What has become more evident in the time since that publication are the strategies and processes principals must implement in order to create high-performing PLCs in their schools. This book is intended to provide clarity regarding specific, research-based, and actionable steps you can take to develop and lead a PLC.

> Visit **go.solution-tree.com/plcbooks** to see "Why Is Principal Leadership So Important?" for a sampling of the research on principal leadership.

It may seem from the progression of the chapters in this book that the PLC process is sequential and linear: first do this, then do that, and so on. In reality, however, transforming a school into a PLC is neither sequential nor linear. In most instances you must address several issues simultaneously and you will almost inevitably need to return to correct or improve upon your initial efforts. Therefore, do not think of this book as providing you with a recipe, but rather, consider it a resource you can turn to for ideas as you confront a specific challenge.

Although the ideas presented in this book are grounded in research, we have opted to be more conversational than scholarly in tone. We do, however, provide readers with access to relevant research as well as reproducible tools and templates, all available at **go.solution-tree.com /plcbooks.** Throughout the book you will see feature boxes (like the one above) that refer you to these materials. In addition, **www.allthingsplc.info** is a tremendous free resource for those interested in implementing the PLC process in their school. This site also will provide you with more information on any of the schools we reference in this book, including contact information for readers who have questions for those schools.

Chapter 1 offers strategies for initiating the PLC process and laying the solid foundation that supports high-performing PLCs. Chapter 2 considers the steps principals take in creating the structures to support the collaborative team process. Chapter 3 draws a distinction between groups and teams, identifies the defining characteristics of effective teams, and presents specific tools for helping educators in a school make the transition from a group to a team. Chapter 4 stresses the importance of helping collaborative teams focus their efforts on factors that impact the learning of students. It also presents ideas for bringing new staff onto existing teams. Chapter 5 examines how effective principals monitor the work of the teams in their school and provides teams with the clarity, resources, and support to be successful at what they are called upon to do.

Chapter 6 is devoted to helping a school develop a key characteristic of a PLC: a results orientation. It explores how schools are using evidence of student learning to drive a continuous improvement process that represents the most powerful form of professional development. Chapter 7 provides keys to creating intervention systems that ensure any student who struggles to acquire an essential skill or concept will receive additional time and support for learning through a process that is timely, specific, directive, and systematic. It presents common mistakes that schools are making as they attempt to implement a response to intervention (RTI) process and suggests how to avoid those mistakes. Chapter 8 offers a tool to help principals reflect on the effectiveness of their communication, including strategies for addressing staff members who resist any effort to align the practices of their school with the PLC process. Chapter 9 outlines three keys for sustaining a school improvement initiative. Finally, chapter 10 argues that one of a principal's most important responsibilities is helping others to believe in their ability to accomplish important objectives in spite of the obstacles they confront. It offers keys to creating this sense of collective efficacy among a staff.

What Is a Professional Learning Community?

In order to lead a PLC, principals must have a deep understanding of what constitutes a PLC and what does not. The growing recognition of the potential of the PLC process to impact student achievement in a powerful and positive way has helped bring the term *professional learning community* into the common vocabulary of educators throughout the world. While the term has become widespread, the underlying practices have not, and many of the schools that proudly proclaim to be professional learning communities do none of the things PLCs actually do. It will be difficult to implement the PLC process in schools when the principal and staff recognize what the process entails: it will be impossible to do so when there is ambiguity or only a superficial understanding of what must be done.

Some educators approach the PLC process as if it were a program—simply one more addition to the school's existing practices. It is not a program to be purchased or an appendage to the existing structure and culture of a school but a process that profoundly impacts the existing structure and culture. Others regard it as a meeting, as in, "We do PLCs on Wednesdays from 9:00 to 10:00 a.m., and then we return to business as usual." It is not a meeting. Still others equate a PLC to a book club, as in, "We all read the same book and talk about it." It is not a book club. It is "an ethos that infuses every single aspect of a school's operation" (Hargreaves as cited in Sparks, 2004, p. 48) that calls on all educators in the school to redefine their roles and responsibilities.

The following section, adapted from DuFour and Marzano (2011), attempts to clarify the three big ideas that drive the PLC process. Each of these ideas has a significant implication for educators.

1. The first big idea is that the fundamental purpose of our school is to ensure that all students learn at high levels. In order to bring this idea to life, educators work together to clarify the following.

   › **What is it we want our students to know?** What knowledge, skills, and dispositions must all students acquire as a result of this grade level, this course, and this unit we are about to teach? What systems have we put in place to ensure we are providing every student with access to a guaranteed and viable curriculum regardless of the teacher to whom that student might be assigned?

   › **How will we know if our students are learning?** How can we check for understanding on an ongoing basis in our individual classrooms? How will we gather evidence of each student's learning as a team? What criteria will we establish to assess the quality of student work? How can we be certain we can apply the criteria consistently?

   › **How will we respond when students do not learn?** What steps can we put in place to provide students who struggle with additional time and support for learning in a way that is timely, directive, and systematic rather than invitational and random? How can we provide students with multiple opportunities to demonstrate learning?

   › **How will we enrich and extend the learning for students who are proficient?** How can we differentiate instruction among us so that the needs of all students are being met without relying on rigid tracking?

2. The second big idea is that if we are to help all students learn, it will require us to work collaboratively in a collective effort to meet the needs of each student. Bringing this idea to life requires attention to the following conditions:

   › Educators are organized into meaningful collaborative teams in which members work interdependently to achieve common goals for which they are mutually accountable.

   › Regular time for collaboration is embedded into the school's routine practices.

> Educators are clear on the purpose and priorities of their collaboration. They stay focused on the right work.

> Principals demonstrate *reciprocal accountability* (Elmore, 2004). They provide teachers with the resources, training, and ongoing support to help them succeed in implementing the PLC process.

3. The third big idea is that in order to know if students are learning and to respond appropriately to their needs, educators must create a results orientation. They must be hungry for evidence of student learning and use that evidence to drive continuous improvement of the PLC process. This big idea requires attention to the following conditions:

   > Every member of the organization is working collaboratively with others to achieve SMART goals that are (O'Neill & Conzemius, 2006):

      a. **S**trategically and specifically aligned with school and district goals

      b. **M**easurable

      c. **A**ttainable

      d. **R**esults oriented, that is, requiring evidence of higher levels of student learning in order to be achieved

      e. **T**ime bound

   > Every member of the organization is working collaboratively with others to gather and analyze evidence of student learning on a regular basis to inform and improve his or her professional practice as well as the collective practice of the collaborative team. Team members explore questions such as, Who among us is getting excellent results teaching this skill? How can we learn from one another? What is the area in which our students are having the most difficulty? What must we learn as a team in order to better address that area of difficulty?

   > Evidence of student learning is being used on a regular basis to identify the specific needs of individual students. The school moves beyond using data to make general observations about the achievement of all students. It creates processes to use assessment results to respond to students by name and by need.

   > Educators throughout the school assess the effectiveness of every policy, program, procedure, and practice on the basis of its impact on student learning.

It is imperative to note that the emphasis placed on student learning in a PLC does not diminish the importance of teaching. In fact, the primary reason to become a PLC is to impact and improve teaching. Too many school reforms have swirled around but not within the classroom. Schools have changed their schedules, added graduation requirements, administered required tests, and responded to countless other reform initiatives, and yet, instructional practice in the classroom has too often remained unchanged. The PLC process is specifically intended to create the conditions that help educators become more skillful in teaching because great teaching and high levels of learning go hand in hand.

Before addressing the actionable steps that bring the big ideas to life, once again we return to the question of how you will define your role as principal. All principals work hard. What distinguishes effective principals from their less effective colleagues is that they identify the conditions most vital to the success of their school and concentrate their efforts on creating those conditions. Warren Bennis (2000) asserts that the difference between managers and leaders is that managers do things right but leaders do the right thing. Both roles are important, and effective principals will certainly manage the building well. However, they will also be driven to lead because they recognize the moral imperative that the school serves. They focus on impacting lives whereas less effective principals focus on managing their jobs (Louis, Leithwood, Wahlstrom, & Anderson, 2010). So before pressing on with the rest of this book, take time to think about and ultimately to clearly define your role as principal. If a Martian were to ask you to explain the responsibilities of a principal, how would you respond?

Getting Started

One of the first questions a principal must address to create the conditions that lead to higher levels of learning for both students and staff is simply, Where do I begin? We recommend the following steps.

1. Start with questions.

2. Create a guiding coalition.

3. Build shared knowledge with staff by learning together.

4. Help staff members clarify the school they are attempting to create.

5. Clarify the commitments that are vital to creating the school.

6. Establish indicators of progress and strategies for monitoring those indicators.

7. Develop a critical mass to support implementation and begin taking action.

Start With Questions

It is not imperative that a principal know all the answers to the challenges confronting a school; it is imperative that the principal ask the right questions to help identify and focus attention on those challenges. A principal new to a school should meet with the staff in small groups to ask a series of questions, such as:

- "What do you feel I need to know about this school to be effective as its principal?"

- "What makes you proud to be a staff member at this school?"

- "What are some of the challenges that you confront in the school that make it difficult for you to be as effective as you would like?"

- "What would make this an even better school?"

Small-group dialogues have three benefits:

1. They allow a principal to honor the past efforts of staff members and the history of the school.

2. They demonstrate that the principal values the perspective of others and recognizes they have important insights.

3. They make it possible for the principal to present challenges and ideas in the words of staff members themselves. At the conclusion of the process, a principal is able to say, "I have heard your concerns, and you have helped me to understand the challenges you face. Now let's work together to address those challenges and make this an even better school."

With some minor tweaking, a principal could use similar questions to engage both parent groups and central office staff in similar dialogue. The initial challenges of a new principal include engaging in a fact-finding mission about the school and establishing positive relationships. This good-faith effort to solicit the concerns and ideas of others is an important step in addressing both of those challenges.

These same conversations can also be helpful to an experienced principal. When leaders help staff identify areas of concern regarding student performance and the operation of the school, admit they don't have all the answers, solicit advice and feedback from others, and demonstrate a willingness to act on that advice and feedback, they build trust in their leadership (Kouzes & Posner, 2010). A survey could also be used to gather information on others' perspectives; however, surveys are most effective when they are followed by dialogue that allows for further probing and clarification.

Create a Guiding Coalition

Those who study the leadership of both schools and organizations in general would offer very consistent advice to principals: no single person has all of the energy and expertise to effectively address all of the responsibilities of leadership. For example, one study identifies twenty-one different duties of principals and concludes that the best strategy for fulfilling those duties is for principals to promote widely dispersed leadership throughout the school (Marzano, Waters, & McNulty, 2005). One important step in fostering this shared leadership is creating a guiding coalition.

There are several different ways principals can structure a guiding coalition. In many elementary schools, grade-level team leaders work directly with the principal to oversee the school's improvement effort. In middle schools, department chairs often serve this purpose. Some schools have created a school improvement committee of staff members. Others create short-term task forces that call on designated staff to address an identified problem, develop a recommended solution, and help build consensus for implementation of that solution. Although the format of the guiding coalition may vary, principals who lead PLCs never forget that they cannot do it alone, and so before attempting to persuade an entire faculty to support the PLC process, they identify and recruit highly respected, key staff members to help them champion that process.

Build Shared Knowledge With Staff by Learning Together

A defining characteristic of a PLC is that its members begin their decision-making process by *learning* together. One of the most-important duties of a principal is ensuring staff members are provided with the information and knowledge essential to make informed decisions. Effective principals are vigilant about ensuring people have ready access to the most relevant information and that the group has collectively studied the information before it is called on to make a decision. The assumption here is that when people of good faith have access to the same information, the likelihood of their arrival at similar conclusions increases exponentially. Access to information is the lifeblood of empowered groups.

Initially, this attention to learning together should focus on the school's current reality and the existing knowledge base regarding effective practice. Working with the guiding coalition, principals provide staff members with an evidenced-based profile of the school that helps them surface the school's present conditions with a particular focus on evidence of student learning. The guiding coalition then provides staff with a concise summary of evidence regarding the most promising practices for raising student achievement.

All Things PLC (www.allthingsplc.info) provides very useful tools and resources to assist principals in this important step. Visit **go.solution-tree.com/plcbooks** to download the following reproducibles.

- See "A Data Picture of Our School" for a template to gather pertinent information on existing conditions in your school.
- See "Finding Common Ground in Education Reform" for a sampling of the research on PLCs.
- See "Cultural Shifts in a Professional Learning Community" for information on the cultural shifts that take place when a traditional school embraces the PLC process.

This information should be provided to all staff members. They should also be encouraged to identify additional data they feel are pertinent to understanding the school and to present any research they can find regarding promising practices.

It is important that this process engages the entire staff in reviewing all information. If the principal or guiding coalition does the analysis and merely reports findings to the faculty, staff members become passive recipients of someone else's conclusions rather than active participants engaged in a process to build shared knowledge. If people are to feel ownership in a decision, they must be engaged in the decision-making process. As Stephen Covey (1989) admonishes: "Without involvement there is no commitment. Mark it down, asterisk it, circle it, underline it. *No involvement, no commitment*" (p. 143, emphasis in original).

Too often schools make decisions on the basis of opinion, anecdotes, appeals to mindless precedent, or authority. In a *profession*, however, there is an obligation to seek out and apply the most promising practices. A principal in a PLC will ensure that decisions are made on the basis of evidence rather than whimsy and will engage the entire staff in the review of that evidence.

Build the Foundation of a Professional Learning Community

Building shared knowledge about the current reality in the school as well as the research on the most promising practices in school improvement is a prerequisite for establishing the foundation of a PLC. Think of this foundation as resting on four pillars—(1) mission, (2) vision, (3) collective commitments, and (4) goals, each of which staff members understand and endorse. The mission pillar articulates the school's purpose, the vision pillar addresses *what* the school must become to fulfill that purpose, the collective commitments pillar clarifies *how* each person must act in order to move the school toward the shared vision, and the goals pillar establishes *when* certain specified benchmarks will be accomplished to mark progress on the journey toward the vision. Let's examine those pillars in more detail.

Establish the Fundamental Purpose of the School

Although educators in many schools use the terms *mission* and *vision* interchangeably, those terms represent two different aspects of the PLC foundation. The mission establishes the very reason the school exists, and on this issue, principals of PLCs must be clear and unequivocal: "the purpose of this school is to ensure high levels of learning for all students." When a staff embraces this purpose, every practice, policy, and procedure of the school is assessed on the basis of how it will impact student learning. Every aspect of the PLC process flows from this fundamental premise regarding why the school exists.

Help Staff Members Clarify the School They Are Attempting to Create

One of the intended outcomes of building shared knowledge during the early stages of the PLC process is the creation of a facultywide understanding of the indicators of the most-effective schooling practices. Based on that understanding, staff members are called on to describe what their school will become. Principals recognize that they must know and clearly articulate where they want to take their schools if they expect others to join them on the journey. So they work with the staff to develop a shared vision—a desirable and credible future for the school that vividly describes what people are working to create and what it will look like when they get there.

A vision, however, will influence a school only to the extent that it is shared. The process we have described thus far is specifically intended to result in a shared vision. Instead of saying, "Listen to me, I know what this school must become," a principal is able to say, "I have listened to you, and I understand the school you hope to create. Let's begin to examine all of our current and proposed practices, policies, and procedures to see if they align with our shared hopes for our school."

See "Why Should We Describe the School or District We Are Trying to Create?" for a sampling of research on developing a shared vision. Visit **go.solution-tree.com/plcbooks** to download this reproducible.

Clarify the Commitments That Are Vital to Creating the School

A shared vision describes what a school will become. Collective commitments describe the specific behaviors that individuals throughout the school must demonstrate in order to move the school in the desired direction. These commitments serve two purposes. First, they move the conversation from the discussion of what a staff hopes to create someday to the specific steps that must be taken *today* to bring the vision to reality. Second, articulated commitments help clarify how an individual can contribute to the school improvement effort. Whereas a shared vision focuses on the organization, collective commitments focus on *people*. The conversation moves from "What is the school we hope to create?" to "What must each of us start doing now to move us forward?"

The collective commitments should be specifically aligned with the vision statement, and the principal should model this important step by publicly stating the explicit commitments he or she is prepared to make to contribute to the achievement of the shared vision.

See the Schaumburg School District 54 "Mission and Goals" to download examples of collective commitments for principals, teachers, students, and parents. Visit **go.solution-tree.com/plcbooks** for a link to this reproducible.

See "Why Should We Articulate Collective Commitments?" for a sampling of the research on collective commitments. Visit **go.solution-tree.com/plcbooks** to download this reproducible.

Establish Indicators of Progress and Strategies for Monitoring Those Indicators

One of the most powerful ways leaders communicate their priorities is by creating a process for monitoring progress of those priorities. Effective principals will work with a leadership team to:

- Translate vision statements into specific actionable steps for making progress

- Establish a timeline for when the steps should be completed

- Monitor each step

- Intervene to provide support when staff members are struggling to move forward

- Identify specific benchmarks the staff can reference to keep track of improvement

- Set clear schoolwide goals and ensure that every collaborative team has translated one or more of those goals into a goal for the team that is strategic and specific, measurable, attainable, results oriented, and time bound (SMART)

In later chapters, we will have much more to say about the importance of SMART goals in implementing the PLC process. For now, we will simply assert that if a shared vision is to impact student achievement, principals must help people throughout the school identify and achieve strategic and specific, measurable short-term and long-term goals that serve as milestones of progress toward the vision.

When a staff has answered these questions—Why do we exist? What kind of school must we become to fulfill our purpose? What collective commitments must we make to create that school? and When do we expect to achieve benchmarks on our journey?—people throughout the school have the benefit of knowing why they are engaged in the work they are doing each day. Furthermore, clarity regarding how these questions are answered provides staff members with a powerful frame of reference when they are called on to make decisions. They know decisions that are consistent with the purpose of learning for all, that move the school toward the shared vision, that honor the collective commitments, and that contribute to the achievement of the school and team goals are certain to be supported. Establishing this foundation is just one of many steps on the journey to becoming a PLC; however, it is a vital step that should not be overlooked.

See "The Professional Learning Communities at Work™ Continuum: Laying the Foundation" and "Where Do We Go From Here? Worksheet: Laying the Foundation of a PLC" for information to guide you on your PLC journey. Visit **go.solution-tree.com/plcbooks** to download these reproducibles.

Develop a Critical Mass to Support Implementation and Begin Taking Action

One of the most common mistakes principals make in attempting to implement the PLC process is to delay taking action until every staff member has endorsed the action. Do not confuse a *widely shared* vision with universal support among staff. Principals must strive for consensus as opposed to unanimity. It is unlikely that everyone on a staff will welcome the substantive changes necessary to transform a traditional school into a PLC. Principals who delay action until every staff member is willing to board the PLC train are almost certain to discover the train will never leave the station.

Those who hope to lead a *professional* learning community must recognize that professionals are expected to make decisions based on the evidence of the most promising strategy for meeting the needs of those they serve. In a profession, evidence trumps appeals to mindless precedent ("This is how I have always done it") or personal preference ("This is how I like to do it"). Therefore, effective principals ensure staff members are provided with the evidence to make informed decisions.

They do not allow an individual's preference to supersede a professional's obligation to apply what is considered the most effective practice in his or her field.

Therefore, in attempting to build consensus for implementing the PLC process, principals should work with their leadership team to:

- Build shared knowledge regarding the elements of the PLC process and the research base supporting the benefits of the process

- Engage in dialogue with staff to identify and address concerns and questions

- Encourage dissent and invite all staff to present contradictory research and evidence that suggests the PLC process is detrimental to student learning

- Seek to understand the perspective of those who are opposed to taking action by asking them to share their thought processes and assumptions

- Articulate their thought processes and assumptions, search for areas of agreement, and acknowledge areas of disagreement

- Demonstrate a willingness to compromise on some of the specifics of implementation provided those compromises do not violate the big ideas of the PLC process

Once the leadership team has met these obligations, we recommend a two-part standard for moving forward with implementation.

1. All points of view have been heard.

2. The will of the group is evident even to those who oppose it.

If that standard is met, all staff members should be expected and must be required to act according to the will of the group. Although it is certainly preferable to have staff members engaged in the PLC process out of commitment, actions based on compliance are better than the interminable inaction of waiting for resistant staff members to change their beliefs. Research advises that people are far more likely to behave their way into new beliefs than to believe their way into new behaviors (Pfeffer & Sutton, 2000; Reeves, 2002). A principal cannot stipulate that resistant staff members change their beliefs. A principal can, however, insist that resistant staff members behave in new ways, engaging in behaviors that are essential to the PLC process. If that process proves beneficial to students, provides resistant staff with a positive experience, and leads to better results, changes in their beliefs and levels of commitment are likely to follow. Personal experience remains "the great persuader" and "the mother of all cognitive map changes" (Patterson, Grenny, Maxfield, McMillan, & Switzler, 2008, p. 51).

See "The Professional Learning Communities at Work™ Continuum: Responding to Conflict" and "Where Do We Go From Here? Worksheet: Effective Communication (Chapter 9)" for more information on building consensus and dealing with resistance. Visit **go.solution-tree.com/plcbooks** to download these reproducibles.

Finally, you must identify the specific action steps people within the school will take in order to begin the PLC journey. Don't confuse articulating mission, vision, collective commitments, and goals with school improvement. Addressing these issues will benefit the school only if people begin to *act* in new ways.

The deepest understanding about the PLC process will not occur until the staff begin to do what PLCs do. Don't procrastinate. Work with staff members to make the structural changes that support their new way of working together, clarify the specific work that needs to be done, and begin doing that work.

2

Creating the Structures for Collaboration

Now that you and your guiding coalition have worked with the staff to articulate the shared foundation of a PLC at Work™, how do you bring those words to life? How do you change the traditional assumptions, habits, expectations, and beliefs that constitute the very culture of the school? An important step in transforming school culture is replacing traditional structures with those more aligned to the school you are trying to create, and then supporting the staff members as they begin to operate within those new structures. This chapter will focus on some of the structural issues principals must address to help move a staff from working in isolation or working in groups to working as members of high-performing collaborative teams. Meeting this challenge will require principals to do the following:

1. Organize people into meaningful teams focused on learning.

2. Provide teams with time to collaborate.

3. Ensure campus layout supports ongoing collaboration and shared responsibility for student learning.

When done well, these structural changes sow the seeds that allow a new culture to take root, grow, and flourish.

Organize People Into Meaningful Teams Focused on Learning

If the collaborative team is the fundamental building block of the PLC—the engine that drives the cycle of continuous improvement—then organizing staff into meaningful teams is a critical step on the PLC journey. Note that the PLC process requires teams, not merely groups. As we clarified in the introduction, a team is a group of people working interdependently to achieve a common goal for which each member is mutually accountable. As DuFour and Marzano (2011) stress, "*In the absence of interdependence, one or more common goals, and mutual accountability, a group cannot be a team*" (p. 70).

See "Why Should We Use Teams as Our Basic Structure?" for a sampling of the research on team structure. Visit **go.solution-tree.com/plcbooks** to download this reproducible.

Remember that the work of collaborative teams in a PLC must revolve around the four critical questions:

1. What is it we want our students to learn?

2. How will we know if they are learning?

3. How will we respond when individual students do not learn?

4. How will we enrich and extend the learning for students who are proficient?

An effective team structure will enable each member to contribute to the collective inquiry into these questions and to the shared goal of improving student achievement. Therefore, the question principals must consider when establishing teams is, Do the people on each team have a shared responsibility for investigating and responding to the four critical questions in ways that enhance their students' learning?

If the answer is *yes*, the principal has created a structure to support an effective collaborative team. If the answer is *no*, the members are almost certain to function as a group rather than a team. The following are examples of meaningful team structures.

- **Grade-level teams:** All of the teachers who teach the same subjects in the same grade level are on the same team. For example, the five kindergarten teachers make up the Kindergarten Team.

- **Same-course teams:** All of the teachers who teach the same course are on the same team. For example, the three seventh-grade math teachers become the Seventh-Grade Math Team.

- **Vertical teams:** Teachers are linked with those who teach the same content above or below their grade level or course. For example, in a small K–5 elementary school with only one teacher per grade level, the school could be structured into three vertical teams: K–1, 2–3, and 4–5. In a middle school, the vertical structure might be math teachers from grades 6, 7, and 8 on a math team. The vertical structure is often used in schools where students are grouped into multigrade or combination classrooms. For example, the grade 2/3 teacher collaborates with the other second- and third-grade teachers on the grades 2 and 3 vertical team.

- **Electronic teams:** Although vertical structures may provide a collaborative team for the *singletons* within a school (the sole teacher of a grade level or course), they do not provide grade-level or same-course collaboration. Electronic teams can address that void. Educators seeking teammates beyond their school campuses can turn to their district office, regional service center, or professional organizations to find job-alike partners.

Members of electronic teams use the available technology to support their collaborative process, such as:

> **Email, Twitter, and VoiceThread** for continuing dialogue at times convenient to each individual

> **Google Docs and Moodle** for sharing agendas, minutes, essential outcomes, assessments, data, instructional and intervention strategies

> **Skype and iChat** to facilitate real-time I-see-you and you-see-me dialogue

> **Mikogo** to see each other's desktops, documents, and videos

- **Interdisciplinary teams:** Teachers at the same grade level who teach different subjects can identify an overarching academic goal that the team works interdependently to achieve. For example, an eighth-grade interdisciplinary team might embrace the academic goal of helping all students become proficient nonfiction writers. The team will integrate writing instruction and common writing assignments in all subjects. Members will apply the team's writing rubric to each student's writing, work to establish inter-rater reliability among team members, provide students with consistent feedback regarding their writing, and work together to ensure all students become proficient in the high-leverage skill of nonfiction writing.

- **District or regional teams:** Teachers who are singletons in their schools can become members of district or regional job-alike teams. Team meetings can occur in face-to-face settings periodically, but most often a common block of weekly time for collaboration is agreed on so that team members can remain in their school setting and use technology to facilitate their collaboration.

- **Logical links teams:** Resource teachers, support teachers, and specialists can join grade-level, same-course, and vertical teams that are pursuing outcomes linked to their areas of expertise. A logical link, for example, could be a reading specialist joining a kindergarten team to work with both the teachers and students in building a strong literacy foundation. A special education teacher could join a team of algebra I, third-grade, or primary teachers because the special education teacher shares mutual accountability with the other team members for the learning success of designated students assigned into the course or grade level. Very often, however, resource teachers and specialists serve students in multiple grade levels and courses, and therefore cannot be expected to contribute to every team. We recommend that these teachers select one or two teams each year to co-labor with on a regular basis and that schedules are built to accommodate their participation. They often make these team selections on the basis of case load. For example, the special education resource teacher may have more designated students in second and fifth grades than any other grades this year; therefore, the special education teacher joins those two grade-level teams. Other times specialists may select a team because they would like to become more familiar with the content or because they feel they have particular expertise they could contribute to the team. We recommend that resource and specialist teachers participate in the decision regarding their team assignment. Over time, these teachers can rotate team membership from year to year as case loads and learning needs change.

Does Your School Structure Foster Collaboration or Isolation?

Although there is no one right way to structure teams, researchers have consistently found that the structure that has the greatest potential to positively impact student achievement is one in which members teach the same content, such as all fourth-grade teachers working together on language arts or all middle school math teachers teaching algebra (Gallimore, Ermeling, Saunders, & Goldenbert, 2009; Little & Bartlett, 2010; Stigler & Hiebert, 2009). These structures are well-suited to the shared goals essential to effective teams and provide members with opportunities to learn from one another in ways that have immediate application to their classrooms. Unfortunately, many schools struggle to support collaborative teams because they use structures and assignments that foster isolation rather than collaboration.

For example, in traditional middle and some elementary schools, teachers departmentalize instruction and thereby create multiple singletons in which one teacher is solely responsible for teaching a particular subject area for all of the students of a grade level. In these schools, even if teachers have time to meet with their grade-level colleagues, they struggle to engage in meaningful collaboration because no two teachers share a common curriculum. This structure typically leaves the four critical questions of learning to individual teachers to resolve. Furthermore, the lack of a common curriculum makes common assessments and systematic intervention—fundamental elements of the PLC process—much more difficult to implement.

Before assigning these teachers into vertical, electronic teams, or even interdisciplinary teams, principals should consider whether or not teaching assignments can be altered to foster school-based collaboration rather than isolation. For example, imagine a small seven- and eighth-grade middle school that employs two science teachers. Traditionally, one teaches five sections of seventh-grade science, and the other teaches five sections of eighth-grade science. The two science teachers continue to teach three sections of their current grade level and begin to teach two sections each of their colleague's grade level. For example, see table 2.1.

Table 2.1: Sample Traditional Middle School Schedule

Block	Teacher 1	Teacher 2
First	Seventh	Eighth
Second	Seventh	Eighth
Third	Individual and team planning	Individual and team planning
Fourth	Lunch	Lunch
Fifth	Eighth	Seventh
Sixth	Eighth	Seventh
Seventh	Seventh	Eighth

Once these teachers have content in common, they can begin to have ownership of the science program in their school, not just their grade level, and they can take collective responsibility for the success of all students in science. When the science team establishes a results-oriented goal for student learning at each grade level, the teachers are in a position to begin to work interdependently to achieve the common student learning goals for which they are mutually accountable.

When principals create artificial teams—allowing teachers to join teams based on personal friendships or assigning people into teams that have no shared responsibility for student learning—they do great damage to the collaborative process. Principals must make certain the team structure brings people together who have a shared responsibility to ensure high levels of learning for students they collectively serve.

Provide Teams With Time to Collaborate

If principals hope to foster a collaborative culture, it is imperative that they create schedules that provide time for teachers to co-labor with their teammates. One of the ways in which leaders demonstrate the priorities of their organization is the allocation of resources. In schools, one of the most precious resources—second only to human resources—is time. Some districts provide time for teachers to collaborate through the use of early dismissal or late start days for students, allowing for collaboration while the students are off campus. In many communities, however, changing school schedules is not an option because of busing issues, custodial care, budget constraints, or state mandates regarding instructional minutes each day. Therefore, principals must be creative in finding ways to provide time for teachers to collaborate while students are at school without increasing costs or losing significant amounts of instructional time.

The following list is not meant to be comprehensive, but is merely intended to illustrate some of the steps schools and districts have taken to create the prerequisite time for collaboration. See DuFour, DuFour, Eaker, and Many (2010) for more information.

- **Common preparation:** Build the master schedule to provide daily common preparation periods for teachers of the same grade level, course, or department. Each team should then designate at least one day each week to engage in collaborative rather than individual planning.

- **Parallel scheduling:** Schedule common preparation time by assigning the specialists— physical education teachers, librarians, music teachers, art teachers, instructional technologists, guidance counselors, foreign language teachers, and so on—to provide lessons to students across an entire grade level at the same time each day. Each team designates one day each week for collaborative planning. Some schools build back-to-back specials classes into the master schedule on each team's designated collaborative day, thus creating an extended block of time for teams to meet. Figures 2.1 through 2.3 (pages 20–22) are examples of parallel schedules.

Time	Monday	Tuesday	Wednesday	Thursday	Friday
8:15–8:40	Student arrival (breakfast, Buddy Reading, morning work, and take-in procedures)				
8:40–8:50	Tardy bell, morning announcements, and start of instructional day				
Specials / 10:30–11:15	*(see specials detail below)*				
11:25–12:15	Lunch and recess				
3:05–3:15	Afternoon announcements and student dismissal				

Specials detail (10:30–11:15)

Day	Lib	Tech	Art	Music	PE
Monday		5-A	5-B	5-C	5-D
Tuesday	5-D		5-A	5-B	5-C
Wednesday	5-C	5-D		5-A	5-B
Thursday	5-B	5-C	5-D		5-A
Friday	5-A	5-B	5-C	5-D	

Lib = Library; Tech = Technology; PE = Physical Education.

Figure 2.1: Sample fifth-grade master schedule (four classes: 5-A, 5-B, 5-C, 5-D) for specials instruction and lunch.

Time	Monday	Tuesday	Wednesday	Thursday	Friday
8:15–8:40	Student arrival (breakfast, Buddy Reading, morning work, and take-in procedures)				
8:40–8:50	Tardy bell, morning announcements, and start of instructional day				
8:50–10:30	MATH				
Specials 10:30–11:15	*(see specials detail below)*				
11:25–12:15	Lunch and recess				
12:15–1:00	SCIENCE				
1:00–1:50	SOCIAL STUDIES AND LANGUAGE ARTS				
1:50–3:00	LANGUAGE ARTS				
2:20–3:00	INTERVENTION AND ENRICHMENT				
3:05–3:15	Afternoon announcements and student dismissal				

Specials detail (10:30–11:15):

Day	Lib	Tech	Art	Music	PE
Monday		5-A	5-B	5-C	5-D
Tuesday	5-D		5-A	5-B	5-C
Wednesday	5-C	5-D		5-A	5-B
Thursday	5-B	5-C	5-D		5-A
Friday	5-A	5-B	5-C	5-D	

Lib = Library; Tech = Technology; PE = Physical Education.

Figure 2.2: Sample fifth-grade master instructional schedule completed by the fifth-grade team, in accordance with their district guidelines for allocating instructional minutes to each subject.

Time	Monday	Tuesday	Wednesday	Thursday	Friday
8:15–8:40	Student arrival (breakfast, Buddy Reading, morning work, and take-in procedures)				
8:40–8:50	Tardy bell, morning announcements, and start of instructional day				
10:50–11:25			Lib 1 Music 2 PE K		
Specials	Lib 1 Music K PE 2	Lib 2 Music K PE 1			
11:30–12:05			Lib K Music 1 PE 2	Tech 2 Art K PE 1	Tech 1 Art 2 PE K
12:10–12:50	Lunch for grades K–2				
3:00–3:10	Afternoon announcements and student dismissal				

Lib = Library; Tech = Technology; PE = Physical Education.

Note: Primary students attend two different specials classes each Wednesday morning while the primary team collaborates.

Figure 2.3: Sample primary-team schedule for specials instruction and lunch.

A creative twist on parallel scheduling happens every week at Jeffreys Grove Elementary School in Raleigh, North Carolina, where students enjoy a full range of specials classes each week. Twice each month, however, students from each grade level participate in Fun Fridays, a ninety-minute program that the team of specials teachers collaboratively designs and teaches. The curriculum for Fun Fridays includes character education, team-building activities, creative explorations, interdisciplinary academic activities, concert and performance rehearsals, and fitness programs. Grade-level teams use this time to collaborate about student learning in the core curricular areas. Specials teachers use designated collaborative planning periods each month to prepare for each grade level's upcoming Fun Friday lessons.

- **Adjusted start and end time of contractual day:** Members of a team, department, or an entire faculty agree to begin their workday early or extend their workday by a few minutes one day each week to gain collaborative team time. In exchange for adding time to one end of the workday, teachers are compensated by being able to arrive later or leave earlier at the other end of the work day.

Parma Elementary School in Parma, Michigan, serves as an example. Parallel scheduling is used to provide grade-level teachers with common preparation periods during the school day, but the staff members realized during the first year of their PLC journey that they needed more time to look at student work and student achievement data, create common assessments, and plan for interventions and enrichment. The student day begins at 8:35 a.m., and the teacher contractual day begins at 8:25 a.m. At 8:00 a.m. every Wednesday, however, teachers begin collaborative team meetings. When students arrive at 8:35 a.m., they report to the gymnasium for an assembly until 9:00 a.m., so teachers have an entire hour to meet.

Principal Sue Haney coordinates and supervises the weekly assembly, and paraprofessionals, the social worker, the physical education teacher, and one other activity teacher (art, music, or character education) assist her.

The assembly topic varies. At times, the school invites community resources and other special guests to speak to the students during these assemblies, and about every other month, the high school drama students perform skits for the students related to a character education topic they have studied. Principal Haney also uses the assemblies to announce students who are celebrating birthdays that week and students recognized by their classroom teachers for commendations. As she describes the assembly:

> I have found that I actually love this time to connect with the kids. I love to celebrate them in front of their peers, and it has provided the perfect time to discuss any issues we may be having or do some rule reminders. Sometimes I read to them, we discuss issues at school or my pet peeve for the week, we sing and dance, and discuss good character, bullying, bucket dipping, and so on. Right from the beginning, my willingness to take the students for assembly showed my commitment to the PLC process. The teachers value that time, and it has allowed them to collaborate and work together on a consistent basis with a very focused purpose.

Note that this practice does not result in a significant loss of instructional time. The classroom teachers adjust their morning work schedule to begin instruction soon after students return to their classrooms, and time allotted for specials classes is reduced by five minutes on Wednesdays. The assembly has the support of the faculty and community because they know students are engaging in meaningful activities.

During the 2010–2011 school year, the Parma district implemented a one-hour early release for all schools in the district once each week to provide teachers with an hour for collaboration. The faculty and students at Parma Elementary didn't want to give up the morning assemblies just because the district scheduled the early-release hour. Additionally, believe it or not, Principal Haney didn't want to give up her time with the Parma students! She continues to lead the Wednesday morning assembly, but alternates between primary grades (K–2) one week and upper elementary grades 3–5 the next week. As a result, the grade-level teams still have that extra hour of collaborative team time every other week along with the time provided by their district during early release every week.

- **Shared classes:** Teachers across two different grade levels or courses combine their students into one class for instruction. While one teacher or team instructs the students during that period or supervises *buddy time*—older students reading, writing, practicing math facts, and so on with their younger buddies—the other team engages in collaborative work. The teams alternate instructing and supervising and collaborating to provide equity in learning time for students and teams.

- **Group activities, events, or testing:** Teams of teachers coordinate activities that require supervision of students rather than instructional expertise (for example, videos, resource lessons, read-alouds, assemblies, whole-class testing). Administrators, instructional assistants, and other staff are assigned to instruct and supervise students while the teachers engage in team collaboration.

- **Banking time:** Over a designated period of days, instructional minutes are extended beyond the required school day. After banking the desired number of minutes on designated days, the instructional day ends early to allow for faculty collaboration and student enrichment. In a middle school, for example, the traditional instructional day ends at 3:00 p.m., students board buses at 3:20 p.m., and the teacher contractual day ends at 3:30 p.m. The faculty decides to extend the instructional day until 3:10 p.m. By teaching an extra ten minutes nine days in a row, they bank ninety minutes. On the tenth day, instruction stops at 1:30 p.m., and the entire faculty has collaborative team time for two hours. The students remain on campus and engage in clubs, enrichment activities, and assemblies that a variety of parent and community partners sponsor and the school's nonteaching staff co-supervise.

- **In-service and faculty meeting time:** Schedule extended time for teams to work together on staff development days and during faculty meeting time. Rather than requiring staff to attend a traditional whole-staff in-service session or sit in a faculty meeting while directives and calendar items are read to highly educated professionals, shift the focus and use of these days or meetings so members of teams have extended time to learn with and from each other.

Ensure Campus Layout Supports Ongoing Collaboration and Shared Responsibility for Student Learning

Effective leaders not only consider people and time as precious resources, but they also allocate space and materials to make the best use of those resources. For example, the arrangement of physical space can either encourage or impede interaction in a school. Social psychologists have confirmed the power of *propinquity*—the tendency for people to form stronger relationships with those who are in close physical proximity to them (Patterson et al., 2008). Therefore, principals who expect people to work together interdependently as members of collaborative teams arrange (or rearrange) classrooms and offices to ensure team members work near one another.

We have heard from teachers whose principal urged them to work together collaboratively, but had refused to create a schedule that would allow them to do so. Although the school had everything in place to implement a parallel schedule to provide time for collaboration on a weekly basis, the principal had refused to implement the schedule because some of the specialist teachers objected to teaching more than one grade level on the same day.

At one point, this same principal had allowed teachers at each grade level to create a designated intervention block during the school day so the team could share students and provide a collective and coordinated response when students struggled. The principal put an end to the practice, however, because teachers in the same grade level had classrooms at opposite ends of the school, and the principal felt too much instructional time was lost as students traversed the school during the intervention block. Of course, the principal might have moved the classrooms next to each other, but one teacher objected to moving her classroom. The principal of this school had placed a greater priority on keeping some teachers happy than creating systems and processes that promoted high levels of student and adult learning. As a result of his unwillingness to align the school's structures with its proclaimed priorities, the principal made it difficult for this school to make progress on the PLC journey.

Collaboration and systematic intervention are essential elements of the PLC process. Therefore, principals must create the structures that align with and support collaboration and intervention. Principals must also recognize, however, that while structural changes are necessary to support the collaborative culture of a PLC, they are never sufficient. In the next chapter, we'll examine how effective principals help teachers make the transition from working in isolation to working as members of a collaborative team.

Transforming Groups Into High-Performing Teams

Organizing school staff into meaningful teams and ensuring members have access to one another by addressing the issues of propinquity and time are essential structural issues that principals must address in a PLC. Changing structures, however, is never enough. In order to build and sustain the culture of collaboration focused on learning and results, principals must provide leadership and support to ensure their faculties use the team time wisely.

This chapter will focus on two important steps principals can facilitate to help transform a group of teachers into a high-performing team.

1. Engage teams in identifying collective commitments to guide collaboration.

2. Engage teams in working collaboratively to achieve SMART goals.

> See "Critical Issues for Team Consideration" for the list of eighteen critical issues teams must address as they engage in the PLC process.
>
> See "Why Should We Collaborate?" for a sampling of the research on collaboration.
>
> Visit **go.solution-tree.com/plcbooks** to download these reproducibles.

Engage Teams in Identifying Collective Commitments to Guide Collaboration

Remember that establishing collective commitments is the third pillar in the foundation of a PLC at Work. Members of the organization agree on and clarify the specific behaviors and action steps each person must take toward realizing the school's shared vision and mission. Establishing and honoring collective commitments—or norms—at the team level are as essential to the success of each team as that third pillar is to the stability of the PLC foundation.

When all is said and done, the norms of a group help determine whether it functions as a high-performing team or becomes simply a loose collection of people working together. Positive norms will stick only if the group puts them into practice over and over again. Being explicit about norms raises the level of effectiveness, maximizes emotional intelligence, produces a positive experience for group members, and helps to socialize newcomers into the group quickly (Goleman, Boyatzis, & McKee, 2002, p. 175).

Therefore, one of the first questions the members of each collaborative team should address is, What commitments will we make to one another to ensure we become an effective team? Articulating commitments at the team level and holding one another accountable to honoring those commitments will not only help the group become a team but also will assist in making the collaborative experience more positive and productive for everyone involved.

See "Why Should We Create Norms?" for a sampling of the research on team norms. Visit **go.solution -tree.com/plcbooks** to download this reproducible.

In our workshops, we often ask people to engage in a two-part dialogue that ultimately leads to a list of collective commitments. In part one, we ask each participant to turn to a partner and take thirty seconds to name a personal pet peeve or behavior that, if it occurs when working in a group, makes for a negative experience. In part two, the participants work with their partner to state a desirable counterbehavior that would eliminate the problem and make for a more effective team experience if all team members demonstrated that behavior. Finally, the entire team considers the proposed desired behaviors. Table 3.1 provides examples of the kinds of pet peeves and collective commitments that might flow from this process.

Table 3.1: Sample Pet Peeves and Collective Commitments

Behaviors That Make for Negative Group Experiences	Collective Commitments That Make for Positive and Productive Group Experiences
Arriving late to meetings or leaving early; members being disengaged during the meeting	Beginning and ending meetings on time, and staying fully engaged during each meeting
Complaining and negative comments	Maintaining a positive attitude—no complaining allowed unless we can offer a better alternative that will improve upon the current condition.
Dominating the conversation; sidebar conversations	Listening respectfully to each other
Freeloading; not contributing to the work	Contributing equally to the workload
Sabotaging the efforts of other team members	Fully supporting each other's efforts to improve student learning
Ignoring violations of collective commitments	Encouraging one another to honor commitments, and candidly discussing concerns when the group feels a member is not living up to those commitments

See "Developing Norms" for a process and a template for developing team norms. Visit **go.solution -tree.com/plcbooks** to download this reproducible.

No matter what process is used to establish these norms, or as we prefer, collective commitments, teams should begin each meeting with a review of their commitments. At the conclusion of the meeting, the team should honestly review whether members honored the commitments. Once or twice each year, each team member should also engage in a more formal process of personal reflection on his or her perception of the team's effectiveness.

See "Survey on Team Norms" for sample statements teams could use as they engage in this more structured opportunity for individuals to provide feedback on the team experience. Visit **go.solution -tree.com/plcbooks** to download this reproducible.

We recommend including team names rather than the names of individuals on the semi-annual survey and having team members use the results to engage in a candid dialogue regarding what is working and what is not working for their team. Many teams use the results to celebrate the positive aspects and achievements of their collective efforts and to identify an area of teamwork they could improve on.

We have found that educators have a tendency to ignore this important aspect of the collaborative team process. They argue that they have always been congenial with their colleagues, and therefore they see no need to clarify commitments to one another. This is a profound mistake. Educators in a PLC must do more than *get along*: they must co-labor. Taking the time to clarify collective commitments about how they will work together and how they will address the situation when members do not honor those commitments is a vital step in building the capacity of educators to work effectively in teams. Do not skip this step! Do not assume, however, that simply establishing a list of collective commitments will ensure that every team will be able to work positively and productively. All teams will eventually experience conflict. Making commitments up front, however, provides each team with a basis for dealing with conflict when it arises. See chapter 8 (page 73) for more information about responding when people fail to honor commitments.

See "The Professional Learning Communities at Work™ Continuum: Building a Collaborative Culture Through High-Performing Teams" and "Where Do We Go From Here? Worksheet: Collaborative Culture" for resources to assist team members in reflecting on the current reality of their collaborative culture, engaging in open dialogue with their colleagues about their perceptions, and planning for next steps on their collaborative journey. Visit **go.solution-tree.com/plcbooks** to download these reproducibles.

Engage Teams in Working Collaboratively to Achieve SMART Goals

The third big idea of a PLC at Work calls on members to assess their effectiveness on the basis of *results* rather than intentions and to use results to promote continuous improvement. The idea of schools and districts gathering data and setting improvement goals is certainly not a new concept. Too often, however, those goals have little impact on people throughout the school. In our workshop we often ask the question, "How many of you work in schools that have identified improvement goals for this school year?" Virtually every participant acknowledges his or her school has goals. When then asked, "If we were to call on you right now to tell us your school's goals, how confident are you that you could do so?" Invariably, very few participants indicate they can articulate the goals for their school. As principal, you must recognize that *schools* do not have goals. People have goals—or they don't. Unless people throughout your school are aware of the goals and are acting on them, you have not addressed this important element of the PLC process.

The second problem schools confront in establishing meaningful goals is the tendency to articulate goals that focus on adult projects or tasks rather than results. Goals such as, "We will integrate technology into the curriculum," "We will implement the new textbook," or "We will increase the use of cooperative learning" are not goals at all. They are projects that represent the means to an end. The end in a PLC, the reason educators engage in these projects, should always be to help more students learn at higher levels. Therefore, goals in a PLC will specifically focus on gathering evidence of student learning rather than adult activities.

Effective principals shift the focus of the staff from activity to results by calling upon each team to translate district and school goals into a team goal that each member not only knows but also owns. In their study of effective teams Katzenbach and Smith (2003) found that the single most important thing a leader can do to help a group become a team with a results orientation is to call upon its members to establish specific, measurable, result-oriented "performance goals to which the group holds itself jointly accountable" (p. 13).

See "Why Do We Need SMART Goals?" for a sampling of the research on SMART goals. Visit **go.solution-tree.com/plcbooks** to download this reproducible.

If a team, by definition, is a group of people working interdependently to achieve a common goal for which each member is mutually accountable, then setting goals is a critical step on the PLC journey. The SMART goal acronym offers a terrific tool for helping teams move forward on that journey. According to O'Neill and Conzemius (2006), a SMART goal is:

- **S**trategic and specific

- **M**easurable

- **A**ttainable

- **R**esults oriented

- **T**ime bound

Setting a SMART goal is a relatively simple process in a school committed to continuous improvement. Imagine an elementary school that establishes a goal to improve student achievement in language arts. Each team in the school is called on to:

- Establish a team goal that is *strategically* aligned to the school goal of improved student achievement in language arts

- Analyze data that help its members establish the current reality regarding student achievement in language arts; collaboratively, members identify evidence of student learning that warrants celebration and the content area of their language arts program in greatest need of improvement.

- Set a *measurable* improvement target that represents higher student achievement than the current reality at a level the members consider is *attainable*; the team members believe they can achieve the target if they work interdependently.

- Clarify the *results* it seeks and the evidence it will monitor throughout the year to determine the progress it is making toward attaining those results

- Identify on its pacing guide or curriculum map when evidence of student learning will be gathered, including a target date when members will examine final results to indicate whether or not the team has achieved its *time-bound* goal

Consider figure 3.1 (pages 32–34), which is from the very first school improvement plan that an elementary staff created as it embarked on the PLC journey.

Comprehensive School Improvement Plan

Throughout the year, the school improvement task force monitored each team's implementation of the PLC process and intervened when teams struggled. Teams frequently gathered evidence of student learning to assess their progress toward the goals they had established. This focus on results enabled the faculty to celebrate the gains in student learning and the improvement in their individual and collective professional practice. It also helped teams identify and respond to student learning needs. By the end of that year, four of the six teams not only met but exceeded the measurable targets they established. They celebrated the progress and established their SMART goal for the next year, raising the learning bar just a little higher, based on the new current reality. The two teams that did not achieve their target did, however, experience some gains. They celebrated the improvement, reflected on what they learned as they pursued their goal, and made an action plan for what they would do differently in the coming year to attain their SMART goal. By working interdependently to achieve their team goal, each team contributed to achieving the school and district goals as well.

District goal 1: We will increase student achievement and close the achievement gap in all areas using a variety of indicators to document improved learning on the part of our students.

School goal 1: We will improve student performance in language arts as measured by local, district, state, provincial, and national indicators.

Team SMART Goals	Specific Activities and Action Steps	Who Is Responsible?	Target Dates	Budget	Evidence of Success
Grade K **Current reality:** Last year, 81 percent of kindergarten students met or exceeded the target score on the District Reading Rubric in May. **SMART goal:** This year, at least 87 percent of kindergarten students will meet or exceed the target score on the District Reading Rubric in May.	**Curriculum** 1. Clarify and pace essential learnings (skills, concepts, and dispositions) in each area of language arts utilizing standards documents, curriculum guides, assessment blueprints, and textbooks.	All instructional staff	**October 15:** Reading **November 15:** Writing **December 15:** Listening and speaking		Lists of each team's essential learnings and pacing guides
Grade 1 **Current reality:** Last year, 65 percent of first-grade students met or exceeded the target score on the District Reading Rubric in May. **SMART goal:** This year, at least 70 percent of first-grade students will meet or exceed the target score on the District Reading Rubric in May.	**Assessments** 2. Develop and implement local, common, formative grade-level assessments to: (a) frequently monitor each student's learning of essential outcomes and (b) provide students with multiple opportunities to demonstrate progress in meeting and exceeding learning targets.	Grade-level teams, principal	**September–May:** Checkpoints at midpoint of each nine weeks; district benchmark assessments at end of each nine weeks		Increased results for all students on local, district, state, provincial, and national indicators

Team SMART Goals	Specific Activities and Action Steps	Who Is Responsible?	Target Dates	Budget	Evidence of Success
Grade 2 **Current reality:** Last year, 91 percent of second-grade students met or exceeded the target score on the District Second-Grade Reading Assessment. **SMART goal:** This year, at least 93 percent of second-grade students will meet or exceed the target score on the District Second-Grade Reading Assessment in May.	**Instruction** 3. Create and implement a master instructional schedule at each grade level to provide protected blocks of instructional time for all areas of the content.	Principal, instructional teams	**August 20**		Common grade-level schedules, faculty survey—January and June
	4. Initiate individual and small-group programs to provide additional intervention and enrichment learning time for students.	Principal, instructional teams, volunteers	**September–May:** Daily		Intervention-enrichment schedule; student records; volunteer log
Grade 3 **Current reality:** Last year, 85 percent of third-grade students met or exceeded the standard on the state's Writing Subtest in May. **SMART goal:** This year, at least 92 percent of third-grade students will meet or exceed the standard on the state's Writing Subtest in May.	5. Provide parents with resources and strategies to help their children succeed academically. Information will be provided through grade-level workshops, weekly folders, parent logs, newsletters, and parent-teacher conferences.	All instructional staff, principal	**September–May**		Number of parents in attendance, study guides, and newsletters

Figure 3.1: Sample comprehensive school improvement plan from an elementary school.

continued →

Team SMART Goals	Specific Activities and Action Steps	Who Is Responsible?	Target Dates	Budget	Evidence of Success
Grade 4 **Current reality:** Last year, 91 percent of fourth-grade students met or exceeded standards on the state's reading assessment in May. **SMART goal:** This year, at least 96 percent of fourth-grade students will meet or exceed standards on the state's reading assessment in May.	6. Utilize a variety of instructional strategies to help students learn all essential skills at or above grade-level proficiency targets.	All instructional staff, principal	**September–December:** Faculty meetings, staff development days, and team meetings		Results on all indicators and lesson plans
	Staff Development 7. Collaboratively study standards and curriculum guides to generate grade-level lists of essential skills.	All instructional staff, principal	**September–May:** Faculty meetings, staff development days, and team meetings		Grade-level lists of essential skills
Grade 5 **Current reality:** Last year, 87 percent of fifth-grade students scored at or above proficiency on the state's Reading–Literature and Research English assessment in May. **SMART goal:** This year, at least 94 percent of fifth-grade students will score at or above proficiency on the state's Reading–Literature and Research English assessment in May.	8. Create a variety of common, formative assessment instruments designed to monitor student learning of essential skills in reading and writing.	All instructional staff, principal	**September–May:** Faculty meetings, staff development days, team meetings, and additional time by team request		Grade-level lists of essential skills
	9. Develop, implement, and evaluate team action research projects to improve teaching and learning. Use information from common assessments to identify staff development needs. Provide ongoing, job-embedded staff development.	All instructional teams, principal	**September–May:** Faculty meetings, staff development days, team meetings, and additional time by team request		Quarterly reviews, midyear progress reports, end-of-year team evaluations, and assessment results

Notice that the school goal was written to ensure *every* grade-level team in the school was called on to improve student achievement because all grade levels taught language arts. Had the school focused solely on student achievement on state test scores, grade levels not included on the state test could not contribute to the school goal. By the same token, a goal to improve student achievement in language arts in a middle school typically exempts other departments from contributing to that goal. If, however, the middle school goals included a target that applied to all subject areas, such as, "We will reduce the failure rate," every team could establish a SMART goal. The point here is that in establishing school goals, principals should make certain to include one or more goals that are all relevant to every team.

See "The Professional Learning Communities at Work™ Continuum: Focusing on Results (Part I)," "Where Do We Go From Here? Worksheet: Using School Improvement Goals to Drive Team Goals," "SMART Goal Worksheet: Third-Grade Team," "SMART Goal Worksheet: Eighth-Grade Math," and "SMART Goal Worksheet" to assist your staff in reflection, dialogue, goal setting, and action planning focused on results. Visit **go.solution-tree.com/plcbooks** to download these reproducibles.

Helping teams to establish collective commitments to guide their collaborative work and set SMART goals that serve as timelines and targets for incremental improvement are just the first two steps teams will be asked to take on the PLC journey. The following chapters will address other vital steps and how principals support collaborative teams in moving forward.

CHAPTER 4

Focusing on the Right Work

If you have worked with staff to establish a common mission, shared vision, collective commitments, and mutual goals, you have laid the foundation of a PLC. If you and the staff have established the structures that support a collaborative culture, you have addressed an essential prerequisite for an effective PLC. If at that point, however, the educators in your building do not focus their collaborative efforts on the right work, there will be no gains in student achievement. One of the most important responsibilities of a principal in leading the PLC process is to ensure all staff members understand the nature of the work to be done and demonstrate the discipline to focus their collective efforts on that work. As DuFour and Marzano (2011) explain:

> Collaboration is morally neutral. It will benefit neither students nor practitioners unless educators demonstrate the discipline to co-labor on the right work. The important question every district, school, and team must address is not, "Do we collaborate," but rather, "What do we collaborate about?" To paraphrase W. Edwards Deming, it is not enough to work hard; you must clarify the right work, and then work hard. Effective leaders at all levels will ensure there is agreement on the right work. (p. 83)

In this chapter, we attempt to clarify the specifics of the right work through:

- Creating a guaranteed and viable curriculum

- Monitoring student learning through common formative assessments

- Bringing new members into the PLC culture

- Providing the collaborative team with a role in the selection process

- Supporting new members

Creating a Guaranteed and Viable Curriculum

Once again, the first big idea of a PLC is to ensure that all students learn at high levels. It is easy for a school to adopt a slogan of *learning for all* to reflect that premise. However, if that slogan is to be meaningful, the people who are called on to ensure student learning must be prepared to address the questions, What is it we want our students to learn? What knowledge, skills, and dispositions are most vital to their success?

The importance of providing every student with a guaranteed and viable curriculum is well established in research. This principle simply means that students will have access to the same essential outcomes regardless of the teacher to whom they are assigned, and that the curriculum can be taught and learned in the amount of time that is available (Marzano, 2003).

Traditionally, principals have attempted to foster a guaranteed and viable curriculum by providing individual teachers with a copy of the state standards, the district curriculum guide, or the textbook series for their grade level. This practice, however, does not ensure students have access to the same knowledge and skills. Teachers can and do interpret the documents differently, assign different levels of priority to recommended content, or simply ignore the documents. In short, it is not unusual to see a huge gap between the *intended* curriculum the state or district established and the *implemented* curriculum that individual teachers teach (Marzano, 2003).

The principal of a PLC recognizes that providing students with a guaranteed and viable curriculum requires more than distributing documents and materials to individual teachers. If schools are to establish a truly guaranteed and viable curriculum, those who are called on to deliver it must have both a common understanding of the curriculum and a commitment to teach it. Remember Covey's (1989) admonition that if there is no engagement in a decision there is no commitment to the decision. Therefore, the principal of a PLC will ensure the teachers on a collaborative team have engaged in a process to:

- Study the intended curriculum together

- Agree on priorities within the curriculum

- Clarify how the curriculum translates into specific knowledge and skills

- Establish general pacing guidelines for delivering the curriculum

- Commit to one another that they will, in fact, teach the agreed-upon curriculum

This process would not occur as an annual event, but would take place at the outset of every instructional unit. The team members would identify the most essential learning for that unit, translate those skills into student-friendly language, establish the amount of time to be devoted to the unit, and promise one another that they would focus their instruction on those essential skills.

Note that this process does not result in the prescribed, scripted lessons and lockstep pacing that are being mandated in some districts. Individual teachers would be encouraged to use the instructional strategies they felt would be most effective in helping their students achieve the intended outcomes. Diversity of instructional strategies would be welcomed and viewed as an opportunity for action research. Although the team would establish a window of time for teaching the unit (for example, "We will devote three weeks to this unit"), pacing within the unit could vary. For example, there would be no expectation that on Tuesday all teachers must be on page 18.

Teachers who attempt to address all of the standards in their state documents will never be able to provide students with a viable curriculum for the simple reason that there are far too many standards to be taught in the available time. Not all state standards are equally significant, and the challenge facing a collaborative team is not, How can we *cover* all of the standards?, but rather, How can we ensure our students *learn* what is essential?

Doug Reeves (2002) offers a useful test to help teams identify the standards that are essential. As they consider a standard, teams should ask the following three questions:

1. **Does it have endurance?** Do we really expect our students to retain the knowledge and skills over time as opposed to merely learning this for a test?

2. **Does it have leverage?** Will proficiency in this standard help students in other areas of the curriculum and other academic disciplines?

3. **Does it develop student readiness for the next level of learning?** Is it essential for success in the next unit, course, or grade level?

Another useful question for teams to consider is, What content do we currently teach that we can eliminate from the curriculum because it is not essential? For example, when our colleague Dr. Tom Many works with schools, he engages teachers in a process called Keep, Drop, Create that he implemented when he served as superintendent of Kildeer Countryside School District 96 in Buffalo Grove, Illinois. Members of each team bring their lesson plan books as a record of what they actually taught—the implemented curriculum—and a copy of the intended curriculum documents that their state, district, or province provided. The teams post three pieces of butcher paper on the wall of the meeting room and label them with one of the three categories: Keep, Drop, or Create.

Topics in the essential curriculum documents that teachers included in their lesson plan books are recorded on the Keep page. Topics teams identify as essential but not addressed in a teacher's lesson plan book are listed on the Create page. Finally, topics teachers included in their lesson plan books but are not reflected in the essential curriculum documents are put on the Drop page. As teachers engage in this activity over time, they become more clear, more consistent, and more confident in their response to the question, What must our students know and be able to do as a result of this unit we are about to teach? (DuFour et al., 2010).

In most elementary schools, a single teacher is responsible for teaching multiple subject areas—reading, writing, mathematics, science, and social studies. A school that is just beginning to implement the PLC process should not make the mistake of attempting to establish a guaranteed curriculum for all grade levels and subject areas simultaneously. We recommend that the entire school focus its initial collective effort on one subject area and maintain that focus until staff members see evidence that it is having a positive impact on student achievement. At that point, the school could add a second subject to the process, and over time, address all of them.

Here is a simple test to determine if you are providing students with access to a guaranteed and viable curriculum. If a parent wanted assurance that his or her child will have access to the same essential knowledge and skills regardless of the teacher to whom the child is assigned, how confident are you in giving that assurance? Are you certain that the teachers in your school have worked together to clarify and actually teach the most-essential learnings for each unit of instruction?

See "Why Should We Ensure Students Have Access to a Guaranteed and Viable Curriculum?" for a sampling of the research on a guaranteed and viable curriculum. Visit **go.solution-tree.com/plcbooks** to download this reproducible.

Monitoring Student Learning Through Common Formative Assessments

A school committed to helping all students learn at high levels will engage in a collective effort to monitor each student's learning on an ongoing basis. This careful monitoring will certainly include continuous monitoring in the classroom as part of the instructional process. Effective teachers are skillful in minute-by-minute checks for student understanding as they are teaching and make adjustments in their instruction based on that monitoring. There are times, however, that a teacher stops to gather more comprehensive information about student learning through a more formal assessment process. In a PLC, this process will include common formative assessments that the collaborative team creates as members collectively address the question, How do we know if our students are learning? These team-based common assessments help to ensure that the guaranteed curriculum is not only being taught to students but, more importantly, is being learned by students.

Common assessments gather information on students pursuing the same curriculum by using the same instruments and criteria. If, for example, the assessment is a multiple-choice test, students take the same test. If the assessment is performance based (such as individual reading inventories, writing assignments, oral presentations, or projects), each student's performance is assessed using the same criteria, typically a common scoring rubric that the team developed. Performance-based assessments also require teachers to practice applying the agreed-on criteria for determining the quality of student work until members have established inter-rater reliability—which simply means they assess the work consistently. Teams must utilize a balanced approach to assessment. They should not use only one assessment tool or strategy but should determine the strategy that will provide the best evidence of student learning for a particular intended outcome.

Most assessment experts (for example, Black, Harrison, Lee, Marshall, & Wiliam, 2004; Popham, 2008; Stiggins & DuFour, 2009) draw a distinction between summative and formative assessments. A summative assessment is used to determine whether or not a student has acquired the intended learning by a specific deadline so the teacher can assign a final grade or score. State tests are examples of assessments that are used for a summative purpose. Formative assessments are part of a process to inform both teachers and students of an individual student's progress toward mastery of an essential skill. These assessments present the teacher and student with information on the status of student learning so that steps can be taken to improve on that learning. Students are then given another opportunity to demonstrate that they have learned. One way to distinguish between summative and formative assessment is that the former is used so students can *prove* that they have learned while the latter is used so that students can *improve* upon what they are *learning*.

> See "Why Should We Use Formative Assessments?" for a sampling of the research on formative assessment.
>
> See "Why Should We Use Common Assessments?" for a sampling of the research on common assessment.
>
> Visit **go.solution-tree.com/plcbooks** to download these reproducibles.

In a PLC, collaborative teams of teachers gather ongoing evidence of student learning through common formative assessments, and then use that evidence in four ways:

1. To inform each teacher of individual students who need intervention because they are struggling to learn or who need enrichment because they are already proficient

2. To inform students of the next steps they must take in their learning

3. To inform each member of the team of his or her individual strengths and weaknesses in teaching particular skills, so each member can provide or solicit help from colleagues on the team

4. To inform the team of areas in which many students are struggling so that the team can develop and implement better strategies for teaching those areas

We will address how teams use the results of common formative assessments more fully in chapter 6. At this point, however, we want to stress that until collaborative teams have agreed on a guaranteed curriculum, developed frequent common formative assessments to monitor each student's learning, and used the results of the assessments for the four preceding purposes, the school is not yet functioning as a PLC. Using evidence of student learning to better meet the needs of individual students and to inform and improve team members' professional practice is the most essential work of a PLC, and as principal, it is your responsibility to ensure that the teams in your school are doing this work.

> See "The Professional Learning Communities at Work™ Continuum: Learning as Our Fundamental Purpose (Part I)," "Where Do We Go From Here? Worksheet: Clearly Defined Outcomes," and "Where Do We Go From Here? Worksheet: Monitoring Each Student's Learning" for information to guide your next steps on the PLC journey. Visit **go.solution-tree.com/plcbooks** to download these reproducibles.

Bringing New Members Into the PLC Culture

Bringing new staff into the PLC represents both a wonderful opportunity to strengthen the school and the challenge of integrating new members into existing collaborative teams. If a team has worked diligently to establish collective commitments, identify a SMART goal, develop a guaranteed and viable curriculum, and craft and implement common assessments, how does the appearance of a new member impact the work it has accomplished? In the remainder of this chapter, we offer suggestions for taking advantage of the opportunity while avoiding the potential for disrupting a team.

The hiring process offers principals a powerful platform for communicating the school's purpose and priorities and for assessing a candidate's fit with the PLC culture. Determining that fit will require more than generic questions that reveal little about the person. For example, if a principal asks, "Do you believe all students can learn?," virtually every candidate will answer in the affirmative. Effective questioning will probe to establish the underlying assumptions and beliefs that the individual brings to the job. Therefore, a principal might work with teacher leaders to generate a list of questions that they feel will give them insights regarding the degree to which a candidate is likely to embrace the three big ideas of the PLC process. Here we present some sample questions for each big idea.

First big idea: The purpose of our school is to ensure that all students learn rather than are taught.

- I'm going to present you with four statements. Which is closest to your personal philosophy? *I believe all students can learn . . .*

    a. Based on their ability

    b. If they take advantage of the opportunities we give them to learn

    c. Something, but it is more important that we create a warm and caring environment than fixate on academic achievement

    d. And we should be committed to doing whatever it takes to ensure all students learn at high levels

- If at the end of the first semester, you discovered that 50 percent of your students were failing to demonstrate proficiency, would it trouble you? (How about 25 percent, 15 percent, 10 percent, or 2 percent?)

- We have all run into a student who simply does not want to work but is not a behavior problem and is not interfering with the learning of others. How have you responded to that student?

- Imagine that one of your colleagues states that there is little a teacher can do to help a student who is just not interested in learning. Would you respond and, if so, how would you respond?

- How do you respond to this assertion: "The major causes of learning do not fall within the teacher's sphere of influence. Student learning will be determined primarily by factors such as innate ability, parental support, the socioeconomic conditions in which the student lives, and the beliefs and behaviors of the student's peer group."

- What is your reaction to this statement? "Students have the right to fail and should suffer the consequences of failure if they don't work hard enough to succeed."

Second big idea: If we are to help all students learn, we must work collaboratively and collectively.

- Which of these statements is closest to your personal philosophy?

  › Teachers are professionals who deserve wide-ranging autonomy regarding what to teach, how to teach, how to assess, and how to run their classrooms. I would not presume to advise another teacher on how he could improve his teaching, and I would not be receptive to a teacher offering unsolicited advice to me.

  › The challenge of helping all students learn demands a collaborative and coordinated effort. Teachers need to stop thinking in terms of *my kids* and *your kid*s and work interdependently to promote the success of *our kids*.

- Have you ever been part of a group or team that led to better results and a more satisfying professional experience for its members? Describe the experience. Now think of another time when you were part of a group or team and it was a negative experience. What factors contributed to the difference?

- If you were assigned to a teaching team and encouraged to collaborate, on what questions or issues do you believe the team should focus its efforts?

- Is there a difference between a group and a team? Is the relationship you have with your current colleagues best described as a group or a team?

Third big idea: It is important to focus on results rather than intentions.

- What is your understanding of the term *formative assessment*? Can you cite examples of when and how you have used formative assessment in your teaching experience?

- What is your reaction to this statement: "Teachers of the same course or grade level should use common assessments so each member of the team can determine the achievement of his or her students compared to other students attempting to acquire the same knowledge and skills."

- What is your reaction to the statement: "Teachers and students benefit when evidence of student learning is easily accessible and openly shared among members of the teaching team."

- Have you ever collaborated with teachers to establish criteria to judge the quality of student work and then practiced applying the criteria to examples of student work to ensure each teacher was providing consistent feedback? What is your reaction to that process?

- If at the end of your first year of teaching at this school I ask you to provide me with evidence of your effectiveness, what would you present?

Providing the Collaborative Team With a Role in the Selection Process

A principal who hopes to model a school's commitment to the PLC process and the important role of the collaborative team within that process should consider including the team in interviewing candidates. For example, the principal could narrow the field to two viable candidates, have the team interview the candidates, and then ask the team members to offer their perspectives on the strengths and weaknesses of each. If the principal wanted to emphasize the school's belief in the importance of effective instruction, candidates would also be asked to teach a lesson that the team and principal could observe as part of the selection process.

The selection process should establish the clear expectation that the applicant, if hired, will be expected *to honor and support the past work of the team*. The team should present the candidate with a copy of its collective commitments and SMART goal and ask if he or she would be comfortable honoring the commitments and feel capable of contributing to the goal. If the team has established its guaranteed curriculum and a series of common formative assessments, it should present the candidate with copies of those documents and ask for a reaction. The principal should make it clear that if the applicant chooses to join the team, he or she will be expected to contribute to and build on what the team has done rather than expect the team to reinvent itself to accommodate the new member.

Supporting New Members

Once a new staff member joins the faculty, the collaborative team process is the best structure for helping that person have a positive experience in the school. A longitudinal study of teacher retention found that traditional school cultures with norms that value individual autonomy over professional interaction exacerbate the loss of self-efficacy of teachers and lead to high levels of teacher turnover (Johnson & Kardos, 2007). The same study found that assigning a specific mentor to a new teacher does nothing to improve a teacher's satisfaction or retention. Conversely, the inclusion and support of a collaborative culture in which teachers enjoy ongoing, structured dialogue about professional practice not only have a powerful impact on the retention, satisfaction, and self-efficacy of new teachers but also provide a process for the constant renewal of veteran teachers.

5

Demonstrating Reciprocal Accountability in a Professional Learning Community

Imagine that as principal you have been successful in implementing each step on the PLC journey that we have identified thus far. You have established a guiding coalition and built shared knowledge with your staff on the current reality of your school. You have clarified the rationale for implementing the PLC process. Staff members have articulated the mission and vision of their school, have made collective commitments to align their behavior and practices with that vision, and have established SMART goals to monitor their progress on the PLC journey. You have helped to clarify the work that must serve as the very heart of their collaborative efforts and have created structures to support the PLC process. A solid foundation is in place. What could go wrong? A lot! Effective principals do more than hope teams will focus on the right work and succeed in the PLC process. They monitor the work, intervene when teams struggle, and coordinate the efforts of the guiding coalition to ensure teams are provided with the support they need to be successful in the process.

In this chapter we offer strategies to help principals monitor the work of teams. We also present ideas for helping principals establish the proper balance of pressure and support so that teams have everything they need to succeed in implementing the PLC process and are held accountable for doing so.

What Gets Monitored Gets Done

In most organizations, *what gets monitored gets done*. A critical step in moving a school from rhetoric to reality is to establish the indicators of progress to be monitored, the process for monitoring them, and the means of sharing results with people throughout the organization. Principals who wait until the end of the year to review student achievement on high-stakes assessments make two fundamental mistakes. First, effective monitoring is ongoing. It occurs throughout the year and not merely at year's end. Second, effective monitoring will address not only results (such as student achievement) but also the processes that impact those results.

There is an inherent tension in monitoring the work of teams. On the one hand, principals cannot fulfill their responsibilities to either teams or students unless they have systems in place to identify how effectively teams are working at the PLC process. On the other hand, if the teams are to become self-directed, the principal cannot micromanage their work. This tension is often the source of conflict in schools as teachers and principals debate who will decide how teams will utilize the collaborative time that has been provided. The debate is typically grounded in the question of power: who will have the power to determine the work of the team? In a PLC, however, the question that drives the decision is not one of power but rather one of effectiveness. If the decision is made on the basis of the evidence regarding what work will have the greatest impact on student achievement, the answer becomes apparent. So rather than debating who will dictate the work of the teams, members of a professional community explore which actions have the most positive impact on student achievement and create a process to monitor and support those actions.

Imagine a single school with as few as twenty teachers in which each member of the staff is provided with one hour every week to collaborate with colleagues during their regular work hours. Now calculate the average hourly salaries of the staff. Over the course of the year the district and community will have invested tens of thousands of dollars in those team meetings. Principals must be able to guarantee that educators are using that time effectively in ways that will benefit students.

The best strategy to ensure teams use their collaborative time productively is to ask them to produce, that is, to generate, the products that naturally flow from the collective inquiry of teams who are focused on the right work.

See "Critical Issues for Team Consideration" for the eighteen critical issues teams should consider. Visit **go.solution-tree.com/plcbooks** to download this reproducible.

The form "Critical Issues for Team Consideration" is designed to help every collaborative team clarify the specific issues they must address in the PLC process and to help principals monitor the progress of each team. For example, whether the issue is clarifying the team's SMART goal, establishing the essential outcomes for a particular unit, developing a common assessment, or analyzing the results from an assessment, the team should be provided with a template for presenting its conclusions to the principal according to a specified timetable. Principals would then review these products. If a team was unable to complete the task or presented a product that did not meet the intended criteria of quality work, the principal could meet with the team to help its members complete the task successfully. We further recommend that principals move beyond the ongoing review of team products and meet with each team on a quarterly basis to discuss their work, examine their products, and help resolve any issues that emerge as a result of this dialogue. As teams become adept at the PLC process, they will become more self-directed, and principals can devote less time to monitoring the process. Initially, however, principals must have a procedure in place to monitor and support every team.

Reciprocal Accountability

At the same time that principals must hold teams accountable for focusing on the right work, principals must be accountable to teams by providing them with the time, resources, training, and ongoing support to help them succeed at what they are being asked to do. Principals demonstrate this reciprocal accountability when they:

- Organize staff into meaningful teams

- Provide teams with time to collaborate

- Provide supportive structures that help groups become teams

- Clarify the work teams must accomplish

- Monitor the work of teams and provide direction and support as needed

- Celebrate short-term wins and confront those who do not contribute to their teams

We have addressed the first four of these challenges in earlier chapters and introduced the fifth challenge in this chapter. We will address the challenge of celebration and confrontation in chapter 8. For each step of the PLC process, principals must ask, "What must I provide my teams to help them accomplish the important work that must be done?" DuFour et al. (2010) provide a helpful framework for considering this question. They propose that principals should be prepared to address the following questions for every product a team is asked to generate.

1. **Why questions.** Why should we do this? Can you present a rationale as to why we should engage in this work? Is there evidence that suggests the outcome of this work is desirable, feasible, and more effective than what we have traditionally done?

2. **What questions.** What are the exact meanings of key terms? What resources, tools, templates, materials, and examples can you provide to assist in our work?

3. **How questions.** How do we proceed? How do you propose we do this? Is there a preferred process?

4. **When questions.** When will we find time to do this? When do you expect us to complete the task? What is the timeline?

5. **Guiding questions.** Which questions are we attempting to answer? Which questions will help us stay focused on the right work?

6. **Quality questions.** What criteria will be used to judge the quality of our work? What criteria can we use to assess our own work?

7. **Assurance questions.** What suggestions can you offer to increase the likelihood of our success? What cautions can you alert us to? Where do we turn when we struggle? (p. 2)

For example, apply this list of questions to the expectation that teams will be called on to develop and administer multiple common formative assessments throughout the year. A principal must be prepared to answer the following seven questions.

1. Why do we need to create team-developed common formative assessments? Why can't we simply rely on state assessments, district assessments, or assessments that come with the textbook?

2. What do you mean by a *common* assessment? What do you mean by a *formative* assessment? What resources can you provide us to come to a better understanding of common formative assessments? What tools, templates, materials, websites, and examples can you provide that will help us complete this task successfully?

3. How do you propose we proceed? What process should we use to complete this task?

4. When will you give us time to develop common formative assessments? When do you expect us to develop and administer the first of these assessments?

5. What questions should we focus on as we address this task?

6. What criteria will determine the quality of the assessments we create? How will we know that our assessments accomplish what they are intended to accomplish?

7. What suggestions do you have that will increase the likelihood of our success? What are common mistakes that we should avoid? Where do we turn to for support if we struggle?

A team that is clear on the response to these questions is far more likely to work effectively in the PLC process than a team that is simply assigned a list of tasks to accomplish. We wrote *Learning by Doing, Second Edition* (DuFour et al., 2010) to provide principals with the resources and tools to help teams address each of these questions for each of the eighteen products a team is asked to create as it works its way through the list of critical issues for team consideration we referenced in chapter 3 and earlier in this chapter.

Team Leaders

As we mentioned in chapter 1, no one person has all of the energy and expertise to effectively address all of the responsibilities of leadership in a PLC. Effective principals will disperse leadership throughout the school, and designating leaders for the collaborative team process is an excellent strategy for promoting shared leadership.

Principals can take different approaches to assigning team leaders. Some recruit particular individuals as team leaders based on the respect of their peers or their leadership potential. Others ask the team to select their leader. Still others encourage teams to operate as collaborative groups in which responsibilities such as team leader, recorder, or timekeeper rotate among team members each year. The way in which team leaders are selected can vary, but we have found that leaderless teams do not work well. Someone on the team must be responsible for helping the team move forward with the PLC process.

When a team leader structure is in place, principals can work through team leaders to help promote the success of the team. For example, imagine a principal recognizes that in order for a group to become a team, it must identify a goal that members will work interdependently to achieve. Therefore, the principal is determined to ensure that every team has the benefit of a SMART goal. The principal would meet with team leaders to review each of the seven questions as it relates to SMART goals, answer their questions, and address their concerns prior to team leaders introducing the topic of SMART goals to their colleagues. In essence, the principal is developing the capacity and competence of individuals throughout the school to serve as effective team leaders.

Hope Is Not a Strategy

Effective principals do more than clarify the work to be done and then hope it is done well. They recognize that one of their most important responsibilities is to help the educators in their schools succeed in doing their work at a high level. Therefore, they create the conditions and supports that provide all of the educators in their schools with ongoing, job-embedded, and collaborative learning.

See "Why Do We Need Widely Distributed Leadership?" for a sampling of the research on distributed leadership. Visit **go.solution-tree.com/plcbooks** to download this reproducible.

Establishing a Focus on Results

Keep in mind that everything we have discussed thus far—creating a guiding coalition, establishing clear purpose, shared vision, collective commitments, and SMART goals; creating structures to support collaboration; using articulated commitments and goals to help groups become teams; developing a guaranteed curriculum; monitoring student learning through common formative assessments, and putting a process in place to monitor and support collaborative teams—involves steps and strategies to achieve a single purpose: higher levels of student learning. They are the means to an end, but the end itself is ensuring that more students learn at higher levels.

In this chapter we examine the vital role of team-developed common formative assessment in monitoring each student's learning, driving continuous improvement, and informing and improving the professional practice of teachers. We recommend a protocol to help teams use the common assessment process most effectively. Finally, we argue that using this process to build the collective capacity of a team to provide powerful instruction is more effective in improving student learning than trying to evaluate and supervise individual teachers into better performance.

A Results Orientation

In their chapter in the *Harvard Business Review on Change*, Schaffer and Thomson (1998) draw a distinction between activity-centered organizations and results-oriented organizations. They contend that the former operate under the false assumption that if they implement enough of the "right" programs, improvements will inevitably materialize. These organizations demonstrate a "fundamentally flawed logic that confuses ends with means, process with outcomes" (p. 191). In contrast, results-oriented organizations focus on achieving a few specific measurable goals that reflect the fundamental purpose of the organization. They establish a process to monitor progress toward the goals on an ongoing basis. People throughout these organizations use this evidence to celebrate success and to adjust their practices and strategies when the intended outcomes are not forthcoming. They accept responsibility for results, and they learn from them.

See "Why Is a Results Orientation the Key to School Effectiveness?" for a sampling of the research on a results orientation. Visit **go.solution-tree.com/plcbooks** to download this reproducible.

To illustrate this results orientation in a PLC, consider the standards that have been adopted in Canadian provinces as well as the new Common Core State Standards that have been developed and recommended for state adoption throughout the United States. In a traditional school:

- The central office staff provide principals with a copy of the standards and perhaps a district curriculum guide that has been developed for implementing the standards. The principal, in turn, distributes the documents to teachers.

- Teachers hear presentations on the importance of the new standards.

- Individual teachers review and interpret the standards, assign higher or lower priorities to particular standards, and attempt to teach the standards to the best of their ability.

- Individual teachers develop assessments based on the standards and use the assessments to provide each student with the opportunity to prove whether or not he or she is proficient.

- Individual teachers use the results from the assessments to assign grades and then move on to the next unit of instruction.

In a PLC, collaborative teams of teachers integrate the Common Core State Standards into their routine team process. In a school that functions as a PLC:

- Collaborative teams jointly study the standards and ensure members are interpreting the standards consistently.

- Collaborative teams consider the priority to assign each standard and common pacing that ensures they address each standard.

- Collaborative teams establish common assessments to gather evidence of student learning.

- Each teacher teaches the standards according to the best of his or her ability.

- Collaborative teams use the results from common assessments to—

    › Identify individual students who are not yet proficient in a particular skill or concept

    › Identify individual students who are proficient and could benefit from enrichment

    › Identify areas in which students of an individual teacher experienced difficulty in becoming proficient so that the teacher can explore more effective strategies with his or her colleagues

    › Identify an area in which students in general did not perform well so that the team can address the problem and consider what its members need to learn to improve on the current results

The data analysis protocol in figure 6.1 provides a template for the collective dialogue that takes place on a collaborative team after each common assessment.

Team: _____ **Teacher:** _____ **Date:** _____

The following analysis is based on our team's common assessment of the following essential learnings:

_____

_____

_____

1. Which of our students need additional time and support to achieve at or above proficiency on an essential learning? _____

   How will we provide that time and support?

   _____

   _____

   _____

2. What is our plan to enrich and extend the learning for students who are highly proficient?

   _____

   _____

   _____

3. What is an area with which my students struggled? _____

   What strategies were used by teammates whose students performed well?

   _____

   _____

   _____

4. What is an area in which our team's students struggled? _____

   What do we believe is the cause?

   _____

   _____

   _____

   What is our plan for improving the results?

   _____

   _____

   _____

Figure 6.1: Data analysis protocol. Visit **go.solution-tree.com/plcbooks** to download this reproducible.

Remember that in a professional *learning* community there is a results orientation and a commitment to ensuring the achievement of each student. Thus, actual evidence of student learning becomes the focal point of the work of the team and the basis of team dialogue. In fact, it is unlikely that the collaborative team process will impact student achievement unless members are using actual evidence of learning to respond to the needs of individual students and to inform and improve the individual and collective practice of the team.

Team-developed common formative assessments represent the most powerful tool available to any school that hopes to become a PLC. Here we provide a rationale for making these assessments the cornerstone of the work of your PLC (DuFour et al., 2010).

- Common formative assessments foster efficient and high-quality assessment. Teachers pool their efforts rather than replicating them. If all students are expected to demonstrate the same knowledge and skills regardless of the teacher to whom they are assigned, it only makes sense that teachers would work together rather than in isolation when assessing student learning. Furthermore, as teachers work together to study the elements of effective assessment and critique one another's ideas for assessment, they improve their assessment literacy. An assessment that a team of teachers creates is likely to be of higher quality than one that an individual teacher creates because each member of the team contributes to, analyzes, and critiques each element of the proposed assessment.

- They promote equity for students. When schools utilize common assessments, they are more likely to ensure students have access to the same essential curriculum, teachers use common pacing, and teachers assess the quality of student work according to the same criteria.

- These assessments provide an effective strategy for determining whether the guaranteed curriculum is being taught and, more importantly, learned. Doug Reeves (2004) refers to teacher-made common formative assessments as the "best practice in assessment" (p. 71) and the "gold standard in educational accountability" (p. 114) because they promote consistency in expectations and provide timely, accurate, and specific feedback to both students and teachers.

- They inform the practice of individual teachers. Common assessments provide teachers with a basis of comparison as they learn, skill by skill, how their students performed similar to and different from the other students who took the assessment. With this information, a teacher can seek assistance from teammates on areas of concern and can share strategies and ideas on skills in which his or her students excelled.

- Common formative assessments build a team's capacity to achieve its SMART goals. They allow collaborative teams to track evidence of student learning in a consistent way over time. When the evidence indicates students in all classrooms are experiencing difficulty with a particular skill or concept, the team can target that area for its own professional development. As members develop and implement improvement strategies that solve the problem, their sense of collective efficacy increases.

- Common formative assessments facilitate a systematic, collective response to students who are experiencing difficulty. Common assessments help identify a group of students who need additional time and support to ensure their learning. Because the students are identified at the same time, and because they need help with the same specific skills that have been addressed on the common assessment, the team and school are in a position to implement a timely, systematic program of intervention.

A Change in Adult Practice

However, perhaps the most important reason for anchoring the PLC process in collectively developing, administering, and analyzing results from team-developed common formative assessments is that these assessments are a powerful tool for changing adult practice. Organizational theorists John Kotter and Dan Cohen (2002) contend that the central challenge and core problem of every improvement initiative is *"changing people's behavior"* (p. 2). As a principal, you must ask, "What are effective strategies that I could use to persuade staff members to make significant changes in their traditional practice?" Let's consider some of the possibilities.

- **Sending a staff member to a workshop to learn new practices:** The research on effective professional development advises that simply sending educators to workshops will not change their practice unless they return to a school that provides multiple opportunities to practice their new skills and receive timely and precise feedback and ongoing support. Researchers agree professional development is most effective when it is job-embedded (occurring in the workplace rather than in workshops), collective (engaging a group rather than an individual), systematic (specifically aligned to the goals of the schools and team), and ongoing rather than episodic (Barber & Mourshed, 2009; Elmore, 2004; Learning Forward, 2011; Little, 2006; McLaughlin & Talbert, 2006).

- **Using the supervision and evaluation process to encourage changes in behavior:** According to the results of a national survey of teachers (Duffett, Farkas, Rotherham, & Silva, 2008), three of every four teachers report that the teacher supervision and evaluation process in their schools did nothing to impact their professional practice. These respondents indicated that the process failed to benefit them in any way, and most felt it was merely a formality to be endured. Another study (Weisberg, Sexton, Mulhern, & Keeling, 2009) found that teacher supervision and evaluation did nothing to inform either teacher or administrative decision making in a meaningful way.

- **Pointing out poor student achievement as a catalyst for changes in teacher practice:** A principal who suggests to a teacher that his or her failure rate is significantly higher than other teachers in the building is likely to have the teacher explain that he or she has higher standards than other teachers. The teacher will tend to regard any suggestion that the failure rate should be reduced as an attempt to lower standards. Furthermore, teachers themselves indicate that poor student performance on an assessment does not ensure they will re-examine their practice. Yet another national survey of teachers found that 84 percent of teachers report they are *very confident* that they have the knowledge and skills necessary to enable all of their students to succeed academically. The other 16 percent feel *somewhat confident*. However, when teachers were asked if they believed all of their *students* had the ability to succeed academically, only 36 percent answered in the affirmative (MetLife, 2010).

Thus, teachers are more likely to regard low student performance as evidence of deficiencies in students rather than a reason to change their instructional practices.

Therefore, if these strategies are ineffective in persuading teachers to explore changes in their instructional practice, what will? Richard Elmore (2004) is among the researchers who have concluded that the *most powerful lever* for changing professional practice is *concrete evidence* of irrefutably better results. When teachers find that the students of one or more of their colleagues consistently demonstrate higher levels of learning on skills they have agreed are essential, on common assessments that they helped to develop, they are more likely to explore what practices are leading to those higher levels of achievement.

A second powerful lever for changing professional practice is the positive peer pressure that comes with being a member of a team that is working interdependently to achieve a common goal for which members are mutually accountable. Most teachers will be open to considering new practices if students' performance consistently prevents a team from achieving its goals.

Teachers who work in isolation and only utilize their own assessments of student learning never experience these two levers for change. There is no basis of comparison that reveals better results for some teachers, and there is no imperative to help colleagues achieve common goals. Effective use of common formative assessments is the best strategy we know for providing irrefutable evidence of better results and utilizing the power of positive peer pressure.

In summary, consider this series of conditional statements from DuFour et al. (2010).

1. The key to the ability of schools to impact student learning is the collective expertise of the educators within a school or district.

2. Improved student learning will require improved professional practice.

3. Improved professional practice will require educators to change many of their traditional practices.

4. Among the most powerful motivators for persuading educators to change their practice are (1) concrete evidence of irrefutably better results and (2) the positive peer pressure and support inherent in working interdependently with others to achieve a common goal.

5. The best strategy for utilizing these motivators and improving professional practice is engaging members of a collaborative team in the individual and collective analysis of team-developed common formative assessments on a regular basis as part of the teaching and learning process. (p. 197)

Team analysis of evidence of student learning from common assessments is vital to the PLC process. A principal who hopes to lead a learning community must ensure this collective analysis becomes part of the school's routine practice and that the results are used to respond to the needs of individual students and to inform and improve the professional practice of educators.

See "The Professional Learning Communities at Work™ Continuum: Focusing on Results (Part II)" and "Where Do We Go From Here? Worksheet: Turning Data Into Information" for information to guide you on the next steps of your PLC journey. Visit **go.solution-tree.com/plcbooks** to download these reproducibles.

Teacher Supervision and Evaluation in a Professional Learning Community

Principals in a PLC use the teacher supervision and evaluation process to engage teachers in meaningful dialogue about the teaching and learning process. An effective process will typically include a preobservation conference in which the teacher can explain how the lesson fits in the context of the unit, what students should know and be able to do as a result of the lesson, instructional strategies the teacher intends to use, how the teacher will gather evidence of student learning during the lesson, information about the students, and areas in which the teacher is seeking specific feedback. During the observation itself, the principal focuses on gathering meaningful, objective information about the lesson. In the postobservation conference, the teacher and principal review the information. Rather than simply reciting what he or she liked or did not like about the lesson, the principal engages the teacher in dialogue, asking the teacher to reflect on the information, to assess what worked and what didn't work, and to consider what he or she might do differently if he or she were to teach the lesson again. The focus on the dialogue is improving instruction rather than ranking and rating the teacher.

Principals should use this supervision model on a frequent basis for new teachers, teachers who are experiencing difficulty, and teachers who are attempting to implement new instructional strategies in their classroom. In these circumstances, frequent classroom observations represent a form of coaching and provide the ongoing feedback people need to improve.

It is important, however, to recognize the limits of teacher supervision and evaluation as a primary strategy for school improvement. A common mistake in teacher evaluation systems is to attempt to reduce teaching to a checklist of effective practices, which teachers are then expected to demonstrate in their classrooms. Two of the world's leading researchers on effective teaching, Robert Marzano (2009) and John Hattie (2009), advise that no instructional strategy is always effective, and therefore the only way to determine the effectiveness of a lesson is to gather evidence of whether or not students actually learned the intended outcome of that lesson.

As Marzano (2009) writes:

> In terms of providing teachers with feedback, the focus must always be on student learning and the perspective must always be that instructional strategies are a means to an end. Checklist approaches to providing feedback to teachers probably don't enhance pedagogical expertise, particularly when they focus on a narrow list of instructional, management, or assessment strategies. In fact, such practice is antithetical to true reflective practice. (p. 37)

W. James Popham (2009) argues that the tendency to focus administrative attention on what the teacher does rather than evidence of what students have learned is one of the greatest mistakes made in education in the past fifty years. As he writes, "It is only sensible to focus on the outcomes of instruction rather than the instructional process *per se*. Everyone should be focused on student learning results" (p. 37).

Attempting to improve the school one teacher at a time through teacher supervision is not an effective strategy for schoolwide improvement. Fullan (2010) insists that individualist strategies, no matter how good, will not lead to improved schooling because "at the end of the day, *only collective capacity counts*" (p. 15). As he writes, "better education, strange as it sounds, is not produced by individual teachers working one at a time. . . . Learning is a joint effort of lots of people working together on a given day and cumulatively over time" (p. 71).

A study of the best school systems in the world based on student performance on international examinations found that those systems do not focus on teacher evaluation to ensure accountability (Mourshed, Chijioke, & Barber, 2010). They focused not on what was taught or how it was taught but rather on evidence of student learning. The study also emphasized that:

> The most powerful form of accountability came from peers through collaborative practice. By developing a shared concept of what good practice looks like, and basing it on a fact-based inquiry into what works best to help students learn, teachers hold each other accountable to adhering to those accepted practices. (p. 85)

Therefore, the supervision and evaluation of individual teachers certainly has a place in the PLC process, and principals should use that process to engage in dialogue with teachers, to encourage them to reflect on their practice, and ultimately to improve their practice. However, teacher supervision and evaluation should not be a primary strategy for school improvement. We advise principals to spend less time attempting to supervise teachers into performing better and more time creating the conditions that allow teachers to continue to grow and learn as part of their routine work practice. This learning is deepest when it is collective, job-embedded, ongoing, content driven, and based on evidence of student learning. The collaborative team process is far more effective in creating these conditions than any teacher evaluation process.

7

Responding When Students Don't Learn

Read the mission statements from schools throughout the world and they exude high expectations. They promise that *all* students will learn. However, the best evidence of high expectations in any school is not revealed by reading the verbiage of its mission statement but by observing what happens in the school when some students do not learn.

We have asked thousands of educators to consider the following series of if/then statements.

1. *If* the mission of our school is to ensure all students learn, *then* our policies, practices, and procedures should align with and support that mission.

2. *If* all students are to learn, *then* we must acknowledge that some students will need more time and support for learning than others.

3. *If* some students will need additional time and support for learning, *then* we must create schedules and adopt systematic procedures that ensure those students receive additional time and support in ways that do not remove them from new, direct instruction.

It is ironic that educators readily agree with the first two statements but acknowledge they have not acted on the third. They want to help all students learn, they know some will require more time and support than others, but they have not created the schedule or the procedures that enable them to provide students with something so essential to their success. The failure to address this crucial element in helping all students learn is not the result of a lack of resources or creativity. It reflects instead the long-standing assumption that it is the job of teachers to teach and the job of students to learn. According to this premise, when a student does not learn, it is the responsibility of the student, not the school, to resolve the problem. The traditional culture of public schooling is deeply entrenched in the fabric of most schools. That culture will not be overcome by declaring a new mission statement: it requires living a new mission.

In fact, what happens in most schools when a student struggles to learn will not depend on the school that the student attends but rather will depend solely on the individual teacher to whom that student is assigned. Some teachers work with students before and after school; some do not or cannot. Some teachers take students out of new direct instruction in one subject to provide tutoring in another subject; others do not. Some teachers require struggling students to stay in from recess or to have a working rather than a social lunch period; others do not. Some teachers allow students to retake tests or revise their work until it meets an acceptable standard; others do not. Some teachers keep parents informed of the progress of their students and provide suggestions for how parents can support the learning of their children; others do not. Some teachers have failure or retention rates that are much higher than their colleagues. Some are far more likely to refer a student for special education testing as the other teachers of the same grade level or course. This randomness means that schools are engaged in a form of educational lottery with the students they serve.

Effective Intervention Ensures Students Receive Additional Time and Support for Learning

Teachers are not to blame for this ineffective and inherently inequitable way of responding to students who struggle. If the school has no systematic plan for addressing the problem of students who experience difficulty, individual teachers must add that burden to their already overcrowded plates.

Principals who lead PLCs address this issue by asking the entire staff to consider the question, What will happen in our school when, despite our best efforts in the classroom, some students have not learned what we have deemed essential? The answer to that question must result in a guarantee that these students will receive additional time and support for learning and that this time and support will be:

- Timely, based on frequent monitoring of each student's learning

- Directive rather than invitational

- Specific and precise regarding the needs of an individual student

- Provided by staff members who are most effective in providing help

- Fluid and flexible

- Systematic

Research only supports the mantra "all children can learn" if we add the phrase, "but some will need more time and support than others" (Bloom, 1980; Guskey, 1996; Lezotte, 1991). Unfortunately, time and support are too often regarded as constants in our schools. If a teacher devotes fifty minutes each day for three weeks to helping students acquire an essential skill, every student has exactly the same amount of time to learn that skill. Although teachers can attempt to provide some students with more individual attention and support than others, the demands of managing an entire class of students limit what an individual teacher can do in the classroom. Therefore, at the end of the three weeks, some students have learned and some have not, and the class moves on. Learning is always the variable when time and support are constants. What happens to the students who did not learn will depend once again on the individual teacher.

However, in an effective system of intervention, time and support are the variables, and learning becomes the constant. Some students may not learn the skill in three weeks: they may need four. Some may not learn it in fifty minutes a day: they may need seventy-five minutes. Some may not learn it in a large-group setting: they may need small-group instruction or intensive tutoring.

Effective intervention requires that this *additional* time and support do not remove a student from new direct instruction. Removing students from a class as new skills are being taught to provide intervention only ensures the student falls behind in learning the new skill. Furthermore, that strategy does not provide additional time for learning; it merely changes the location for the learning. Later in this chapter (pages 63–70) we will provide examples of how schools are creating schedules to address this element of effective intervention. Principals must recognize that if time and support remain constants in their schools, learning will always be the variable.

See "Why Should We Implement Systematic Interventions?" for a sampling of the research on systematic interventions. Visit **go.solution-tree.com/plcbooks** to download this reproducible.

Let's consider each element of this effective system of intervention.

Effective Intervention Is Timely

The best systems of intervention monitor student learning on an ongoing basis and respond immediately when students struggle. A study of the world's best school systems found that those systems "take the process of monitoring student learning and intervention inside schools, constantly evaluating student performance and constructing interventions to assist individual students in order to prevent them from falling behind" (Barber & Mourshed, 2007, p. 38). By intervening quickly at the level of the individual students, these schools prevent early difficulties from compounding into long-term failure. This is the antithesis of the wait-to-fail criterion that schools have used to assign students to special education.

The research on reading instruction is particularly emphatic about the importance of timely intervention for individual students on specific skills. When effective instruction and intervention begin in kindergarten and first grade, providing struggling students with as little as twenty to forty-five minutes a day of extra support can ensure 98 percent of students are reading at grade level by the end of second grade. Conversely, a student who cannot read in third grade will require almost constant support in reading to overcome the compounded learning problems (Rebora, 2010).

Effective Intervention Is Directive Rather Than Invitational

An effective plan of intervention will not invite students to devote additional time to their learning or to utilize additional layers of support—it will require them to do so. Students most in need of help in order to succeed are often the least likely to pursue it. Therefore, the school must have a process in place that assigns students to intervention just as it has a process that assigns them to a mathematics class or lunch. This means that the best intervention will occur during the school day rather than before or after school.

Effective Intervention Is Specific and Precise Regarding the Needs of an Individual Student

Effective intervention responds to the particular learning needs of individual students. A teacher who can specify that a student needs additional time and support for mastering the subtraction of two-digit integers helps the system of intervention address the student's specific needs. The teacher who just indicates, "This student needs help with math" does not help the system. Systems of intervention help all students learn when the school is in a position to identify students by name and by need.

Effective Intervention Provides Students Access to Staff Most Effective in Providing Help

Richard Allington (as cited in Rebora, 2010) argues that one of the greatest mistakes schools make in attempting to meet the needs of students is assigning struggling students to the people least qualified to help them succeed. He contends that too often in our schools, no one gets worse instruction than the students who need effective instruction the most. Struggling students need direct instruction from the teacher on the team or the specialist in the school with the greatest expertise in teaching a specific skill or concept rather than being relegated to well-intentioned paraprofessionals, parent volunteers, or teachers lacking content expertise.

Effective Intervention Is Fluid and Flexible

Effective intervention responds immediately to an individual student who struggles and provides additional time and support only until the student demonstrates proficiency. Students are not assigned into specific programs for designated periods of time. Students flow easily in and out of intervention as needed, unlike special education programs in which it is difficult, expensive, and time consuming for students to be identified as eligible for special education services and even more difficult to stop providing those services. The focus of effective intervention is on meeting the needs of individual students rather than complying with rigid rules and regulations.

Effective Intervention Is Systematic

A systematic plan of intervention represents the antithesis of the random, discretionary, and haphazard way in which schools have traditionally responded to students who experience difficulty. When intervention is done systematically, the principal and staff have clearly delineated specific trigger points for specific intervention and have clearly defined roles and responsibilities. As DuFour and his colleagues (2010) write, an effective plan for systematic intervention allows educators

> to guarantee students that they will be given additional time and support if they struggle, to guarantee parents that their children will receive this support in a timely and directive way regardless of the teacher to whom they

are assigned, and to guarantee individual teachers that they are not alone when it comes to resolving the problems their students may experience. The entire staff realizes that there is a collective and coordinated effort to assist students. (p. 224)

Let's consider how different schools have created structures to support systematic intervention for their students.

Intervention in Middle and Junior High Schools

Middle and junior high schools can use a variety of strategies to provide students with additional time and support for learning. One of those strategies ensures that each student's schedule provides time during the day when he or she will not be assigned to a specific class so that the school can provide timely intervention without removing the student from instruction. For example, Prairie Star Middle School in Leawood, Kansas, serves approximately six hundred students in grades 6 through 8. The school offers eight forty-five-minute periods with twenty-five minutes for lunch; however, all students are assigned to a guided study period. Teachers oversee guided study as a supervisory duty, and Principal Lyn Rantz makes assignments very purposefully. She attempts to ensure that a math, a reading, and a special education teacher are available each period and creates a guided study for gifted students that the school's gifted teacher leads.

Half of the students in each grade level attend guided study periods every other day while their classmates are in physical education class. This rotation allows the school to limit the number of students in any guided study to fewer than fourteen students, so teachers can provide them more personal attention. Students who are very deficient in a subject or who need help in more than one subject may be assigned to a second guided study period, that is, one each day. If students continue to struggle despite the extra time and support they receive in guided study, they are assigned to a learning lab in which a staff member monitors their work each day to ensure they complete their homework successfully. Additional levels of time and support are also available for students.

Prior to implementing the PLC process with this system of intervention, Prairie Star Middle was the lowest-performing middle school in the Blue Valley School District. Since adopting the PLC process, the school has become one of the highest-performing middle schools in Kansas.

A second approach to providing time and support for students is to carve out a specific time each day when the school stops new direct instruction to provide intervention and enrichment. Lakeridge Junior High School in Orem, Utah, serves over 1,200 students in grades 7 through 9. It uses a modified A/B block in which students take four eighty-minute classes each day.

The Lakeridge schedule also includes a thirty-minute flex period four days each week. During that period, students who are being successful in all of their classes have access to over twenty enrichment activities, such as Model United Nations, Mock Trial, and Math Team. Other options are more social, such as intramural sports, the video game Dance Dance Revolution, or extended lunch. Students who are not assigned to tutoring are allowed to elect the activity of their choice and, with the exception of a few of the cocurricular programs, they may elect different options each day. As Principal Garrick Peterson explains, "We consider enrichment time as the students' time. They have demonstrated responsibility in passing all of their courses, and so we trust them to act responsibly and choose wisely during the flex period."

For students who are not passing all of their classes or who are failing to complete their work, flex time provides mandatory intensive small-group tutoring until students are successful. Lakeridge reports each student's achievement in every class on a *daily* basis. The very day that a student is found to be struggling, the student is assigned to tutoring.

If students continue to experience difficulty, the school has a variety of other options it will apply. Students are assigned to Counselor Watch and review their progress with their counselor each week. Students can have their schedules adjusted to provide a double block of a subject, a study-skills class, or a guided study hall in which staff members monitor the completion of their work.

Students who fail a class at the end of a grading period are assigned to meet with the teacher of that class during the flex period for the first two weeks of the next term to complete assignments and demonstrate proficiency. If, at the end of the two weeks, they remain unable to demonstrate proficiency, Principal Peterson, counselors, and support staff spend a day with the students in an effort to resolve their difficulties. The school then requires students to stay after school for tutoring four days each week (busing is provided), and at the conclusion of the year, failing students are assigned to summer school to continue working until they can earn their credits. As Peterson puts it, "We tell our students: 'We will give you some choice about when you learn, but ultimately you must learn. Learning is required rather than optional.'"

Prior to initiating the PLC process and implementing this comprehensive plan of intervention as part of that process, Lakeridge was the lowest-performing junior high school in the Alpine School District. Since committing to the PLC process it has been named the best school in Utah in both 2008 and 2009.

Frost Junior High School in Schaumburg, Illinois, uses a creative schedule to provide its six hundred seventh- and eighth-grade students with multiple opportunities for additional time and support. Principal Paul Goldberg and his staff have created a basic schedule that offers nine forty-minute periods. After every common assessment in the core curriculum, teacher teams stop new direct instruction for a few days and assign students into different groups for enrichment, practice, or intervention. Additional personnel such as special education teachers, the literacy coach, and bilingual resource teachers join the team to assist with intervention on those days.

Students who do not complete their homework are assigned to Homework Intervention during their lunch periods. This program functions as a working lunch, and students remain in the program until all homework is completed. The school also provides several student support groups to provide designated students with social and academic support.

On Tuesdays and Thursdays, the school offers yet another structure for supporting struggling students when it shortens each of the periods to create a tenth period for intervention and enrichment. This tenth period follows a two-week rotation as presented in table 7.1. If a student is failing both of the classes that are offering intervention on that day, the class listed first gets priority. Students who are not failing either class can be assigned to tutoring in any other class where they are experiencing difficulty. Teachers can also use this time to provide individual or small-group support for proficient students to deepen their learning.

Table 7.1: Sample Two-Week Rotation for Intervention and Enrichment

	Tuesday	**Thursday**
Week One	• Math • Language arts	• Social studies • Math
Week Two	• Language arts • Math	• Science • Language arts
Week Three	• Math • Language arts	• Social studies • Math
Week Four	• Language arts • Math	• Science • Language arts

Students who continue to struggle to become proficient in reading are assigned into a double literacy block eighty minutes each day. Reading intervention teachers use the additional forty-minute block in small-group instruction to preteach the skills and concepts students will be learning in the next unit of their core curriculum.

The impact on student achievement has been dramatic. The percentage of students able to demonstrate proficiency on the state test has increased by more than 20 percent between 2006 and 2011, making Frost one of the few schools in the state to have over 95 percent of its students proficient in all subject areas. In 2011, the U.S. Department of Education named Frost one of two junior high/ middle schools in Illinois to receive its Blue Ribbon Award.

Although these schools have different schedules, they have several things in common. First, they addressed the question of intervention not as an add-on to traditional school structures but as part of the process to reculture their school into a PLC. At the same time, they were addressing how they would respond when students did not learn, collaborative teams of teachers were establishing a guaranteed curriculum, developing and administering common assessments to monitor each student's learning, and using evidence of that learning to help each member of the team become more effective in teaching the guaranteed curriculum. Second, they recognized that helping all students learn would take a collective effort rather than a series of isolated individual efforts. Third, they acknowledged that some students would require more time and support to be successful in their learning, so they accepted the responsibility to create the schedule and structures to ensure students would receive that time and support.

Intervention in Elementary Schools

Some elementary schools use a model similar to the Lakeridge flex plan as their intervention and enrichment strategy. These schools designate one time each day when the staff attempt to address the needs of all their students by assigning them to intervention, extension, or enrichment groups based on their current levels of demonstrated proficiency in the essential skills and concepts being taught. Although this approach does represent a collective effort to provide students with timely, directive, and systematic intervention and enrichment, it presents a significant challenge. Because staff members are attempting to meet the needs of every student in the school during a single designated time, they find it difficult to provide the intensive individualized support some students require during this narrow window of opportunity. The problem persists even if the school takes an all-hands-on-deck approach in which every member of the instructional staff assumes responsibility for a specific cluster of students with similar learning needs.

This problem can be avoided when elementary schools provide students with systematic intervention and enrichment *throughout* the school day by targeting students in specific grade levels for support at designated times. In this structure, each team—grade level or vertical—designates a specific time for daily intervention and enrichment in much the same way time is designated for daily instruction in language arts, math, science, and social studies. By distributing intervention and enrichment time by team throughout the school day, the school is able to provide more intensive support to smaller groups of students than any model that requires every struggling student in the school to receive help at the same time.

Sample schoolwide and grade-level schedules for this preferred structure are presented in figures 7.1 through 7.3 (pages 67–69) and table 7.2 (page 70).

Team-developed common formative assessments drive this process. After each of those assessments, the team reviews the evidence of student learning and asks the following questions:

- "How should we cluster the students for the next intervention and enrichment cycle?"

- "Which member of our team should take the lead with which cluster?"

- "What strategies and materials will be utilized with each cluster?"

- "How will we monitor and gather evidence of each student's learning during this cycle of I/E?"

During the designated intervention and enrichment time, every student in the grade level is assigned into a learning cluster with peers who have similar learning needs based on the results of the team's most recent common formative assessment. Classroom teachers and I/E Team members (additional instructional personnel who have traditionally accessed individual students for pullout services) now coordinate curriculum and instructional services so that one or more adults take responsibility for a cluster of students with similar learning needs. For example, during I/E time, resource specialists in areas such as Title I, English as a second language, gifted and talented, and speech and language can access the students identified to receive their supplementary services. Classroom teachers and coaches, teacher assistants, and administrators are each assigned one cluster of

Kindergarten	Grade 1	Grade 2	Grade 3	Grade 4	Grade 5
Science 8:50–9:35 (45 minutes)	Social Studies/ Language Arts 8:50–9:40 (50 minutes)	Small Group Instruction for I/E and Guided Reading 8:50–9:40 (50 minutes)	Specials 8:50–9:35 Music, Art, PE, Library, Technology (45 minutes)	Science 8:50–9:35 (45 minutes)	Math 8:50–10:30 (100 minutes)
Language Arts/ Social Studies 9:40–10:40 (60 minutes)	Language Arts 9:40–11:00 (80 minutes)	Language Arts 8:50–10:05 (75 minutes)	Math 9:40–11:10 (90 minutes)	Specials 9:40–10:25 Music, Art, PE, Library, Technology (45 minutes)	
	Small Group Instruction for I/E and Guided Reading 9:45–10:45 (60 minutes)	Social Studies/ Language Arts 10:05–10:50 (45 minutes)		Social Studies/ Language Arts 10:25–11:15 (50 minutes)	Specials 10:30–11:15 Music, Art, PE, Library, Technology (45 minutes)
Language Arts 10:40–12:10 (90 minutes)		Science 10:50–11:35 (45 minutes)			
Small Group Instruction for I/E and Guided Reading 10:50–11:50 (60 minutes)	Lunch/Recess 11:05–11:55 (50 minutes)		Social Studies/ Language Arts 11:10–12:00 (50 minutes)	Lunch/Recess 11:15–12:05 (50 minutes)	Lunch/Recess 11:25–12:15 (50 minutes)
		Lunch/Recess 11:35–12:25 (50 minutes)			
Lunch/Recess 12:10–1:10 (60 minutes)	Math 12:00–1:20 (80 minutes)		Lunch/Recess 12:00–12:50 (50 minutes)	Language Arts 12:05–1:30 (85 minutes)	Science 12:15–1:00 (45 minutes)
		Specials 12:35–1:20 Music, Art, PE, Library, Technology (45 minutes)	Language Arts 12:50–2:15 (85 minutes)	I/E 12:40–1:25 (45 minutes)	Social Studies/ Language Arts 1:00–1:50 (50 minutes)
Math 1:15–2:15 (60 minutes)	Specials 1:25–2:10 Music, Art, PE, Library, Writing (45 minutes)	Math 1:25–3:00 (95 minutes)	I/E 1:30–2:15 (45 minutes)	Math 1:30–3:00 (90 minutes)	Language Arts 1:50–3:00 (70 minutes)
Specials 2:15–3:00 Music, Art, PE, Library, Technology (45 minutes)	Science 2:15–3:00 (45 minutes)		Science 2:15–3:00 (45 minutes)		I/E 2:20–3:00 (40 minutes)
Students Depart 3:05–3:15	Students Depart 3:05–3:15	Students Depart 3:05–3:15	Students Depart 3:05–3:15	Students Depart 3:05–3:15	Students Depart 3:05–3:15

Figure 7.1: Sample master instructional schedule for grades K–5.

Time	Monday	Tuesday	Wednesday	Thursday	Friday
8:15–8:40	Student arrival (breakfast, morning work, and take-in procedures)				
8:40–8:50	Tardy bell, morning announcements, and start of instructional day				
8:50–9:40	SOCIAL STUDIES AND LANGUAGE ARTS				
9:45–10:15	GUIDED READING CLUSTERS 1, INTERVENTION AND ENRICHMENT (I/E) CLUSTERS 2				
10:15–10:45	GUIDED READING CLUSTERS 2, I/E CLUSTERS 1				
10:45–11:00	LANGUAGE ARTS				
11:05–11:55	Lunch and recess				
12:00–1:20	MATH				
Specials	Lib 1-A, Tech 1-B, Music 1-C, Art 1-D, PE 1-E	Lib 1-B, Tech 1-C, Music 1-D, Art 1-E, PE 1-A	Lib 1-C, Tech 1-D, Music 1-E, Art 1-A, PE 1-B	Lib 1-D, Tech 1-E, Music 1-A, Art 1-B, PE 1-C	Lib 1-E, Tech 1-A, Music 1-B, Art 1-C, PE 1-D
1:25–2:10	SCIENCE				
2:15–3:00	SCIENCE				
3:00–3:10	Afternoon announcements and student dismissal				
3:05–3:15	Students depart				
3:10–3:30	Instructional staff planning				

Lib = Library; Tech = Technology; PE = Physical Education.

Figure 7.2: Sample first-grade master schedule for instruction.

Time	Monday	Tuesday	Wednesday	Thursday	Friday
8:15–8:40	Student arrival (breakfast, Buddy Reading, morning work, and take-in procedures)				
8:40–8:50	Tardy bell, morning announcements, and start of instructional day				
9:40–11:10	MATH				
11:10–12:00	SOCIAL STUDIES AND LANGUAGE ARTS				
12:00–12:50	Lunch and recess				
12:50–2:15	LANGUAGE ARTS				
1:30–2:15	INTERVENTION AND ENRICHMENT TEAM				
2:15–3:00	SCIENCE				
3:05–3:15	Afternoon announcements and student dismissal				

Specials (8:50–9:35):

Subject	Monday	Tuesday	Wednesday	Thursday	Friday
Lib		3-A	3-B	3-C	3-D
Tech	3-A	3-B		3-D	3-C
Music	3-B	3-C	3-D	3-A	
Art	3-C	3-D	3-A		3-B
PE	3-D		3-C	3-B	3-A

Lib = Library; Tech = Technology; PE = Physical Education.

Figure 7.3: Sample third-grade master schedule for instruction (four classes: 3-A, 3-B, 3-C, 3-D).

Table 7.2: Sample Weekly Intervention Team Schedule

8:15–8:45	Planning
8:50–9:40	Second grade
9:45–10:45	First grade
10:50–11:50	Kindergarten
11:50–12:35	Lunch and planning
12:40–1:25	Fourth grade
1:30–2:15	Third grade
2:20–3:00	Fifth grade
3:05–3:15	Student dismissal

the remaining students. The students who are currently struggling the most to demonstrate proficiency of an essential skill or concept are assigned to the teachers who have the greatest expertise in teaching that skill or concept. While these students receive intensive small-group and individual support for intervention, the other students are clustered with peers for extension and enrichment of newly acquired essential learnings. Team members frequently monitor each student's response to intervention, reassess those students periodically, and either move a student to the extension group to practice a newly acquired skill, an enrichment group to deepen the understanding of a skill, or to an intensive intervention as that student's needs dictate.

Some elementary schools with few or no additional instructional personnel other than classroom teachers shift their allocation of funds from providing things like after-school tutoring or summer school to hiring additional part-time or full-time personnel. These staff members most often assist with implementing and supervising the extension activities—under the direction of the collaborative team—during the I/E times scheduled within the school day. The candidates often come from pools of recently retired teachers, certified substitute teachers, or new teachers who have not yet been hired for a full-time position. In addition to hiring part-time personnel, these schools also look for additional support from community volunteers, college students pursuing degrees in education, and even college-bound high school interns.

Although the human resources will vary from school to school, one thing is constant. This targeted and specific learning support that students receive during intervention and enrichment time is in addition to—not in place of—receiving new direct instruction each day. Regardless of whether the school is urban, suburban, or rural—or whether a student is designated for general education, special education, or English language development—in a high-performing PLC school, the adults take collective responsibility to ensure *all* students receive high-quality new direct instruction of grade-level curriculum and extra time and support to learn at high levels each day.

The Biggest Obstacle to Powerful Intervention and Enrichment

Principals must recognize the greatest obstacle in creating powerful systems of intervention is not a structural challenge that calls for creative scheduling and staffing, but rather the challenge of addressing the assumptions and beliefs that have characterized the traditional culture of schools. Systems of intervention will be ineffective if educators believe that:

- What they teach, how they teach, how they assess the learning of each student, and how they respond when students do not learn should be left to the discretion of the individual teacher

- It is their job to teach—it is the student's job to learn

- The primary purpose of assessment is to assign grades

- Effective intervention can be accomplished by purchasing new curriculum or computer-based programs of instruction

- Intervention is simply a modified form of special education or a procedure to follow to assign students into special education more expeditiously

- Students should be encouraged but not required to avail themselves of extra time and support when they struggle

The foundation of powerful systems of intervention includes:

- A commitment to help all students learn at high levels

- A collective effort to support that learning

- Effective instruction in the classroom each day

- A process to help each teacher become more effective

- Ongoing monitoring of each student's learning

- The ability to identify students who need support by name and by need

- Clear communication regarding roles and responsibilities for effective intervention

As principal, you must recognize that no system of intervention can compensate for ongoing weak and ineffective teaching or a culture that is indifferent to the success of each student. To be effective, RTI must be part of a larger process designed to create the structures and culture that support PLCs. As Buffum, Mattos, and Weber (2009) write in their outstanding book on RTI:

> The essential characteristics of a professional learning community are perfectly aligned with the fundamental elements of response to intervention. Quite simply, PLC and RTI are complementary processes, built upon a proven research base of best practices and designed to produce the same outcome—high levels of student learning. PLCs create the schoolwide cultural and structural foundation necessary to implement a highly effective RTI program. (p. 49)

Creating effective systems of intervention is not separate and apart from the PLC process—it is an essential element of that process.

Many educators throughout the United States have regarded the federal response to intervention (RTI) initiative as a separate program that should merely be added to the existing structure of their schools. In a PLC, however, educators recognize that creating an effective *process* of intervention and enrichment is neither a program nor a separate addition to the fundamental work of the school. Having a plan to provide students with additional time and support for learning in a way that is timely, directive, fluid, precise, and systematic is an essential characteristic of any school that functions as a PLC.

See "The Professional Learning Communities at Work™ Continuum: Learning as Our Fundamental Purpose (Part II)" and "Where Do We Go From Here? Worksheet: Systematic Intervention" for information to guide your next steps on the PLC journey. Visit **go.solution-tree.com/plcbooks** to download these reproducibles.

8

Communicating Purpose and Priorities

One of the great challenges every principal must resolve is the top-down versus bottom-up approach to leadership. Should a principal use the authority of his or her position to demand adherence to certain core principles and practices in the school, or should the principal encourage autonomy by empowering people throughout the organization to make important decisions? The best answer to both parts of this question is yes. Effective principals reject what Collins and Porras (1997) refer to as the "Tyranny of the OR" and instead embrace the "Genius of the AND." They clearly communicate that certain things in the school are nondiscretionary at the same time that they empower the staff to make significant decisions. As a result, the culture of a PLC is both nondiscretionary (or tight) *and* empowering (or loose). This simultaneous loose-tight culture, also referred to as defined autonomy or directed empowerment, is fundamental to the PLC process.

In this chapter we explore what must be tight in a PLC and how principals communicate what is tight to everyone in the school. We provide a series of questions that a principal can use to assess the quality and effectiveness of his or her communication. We acknowledge it is likely that some staff will object to implementing the fundamental elements of a PLC and offer specific strategies for working with those staff members.

Getting Tight About the Right Things

There are two keys to creating a loose-tight culture that promotes more students learning at higher levels: (1) becoming tight about the right things and (2) clarifying what is tight so that people throughout the organization understand what is nondiscretionary. As we stressed in chapter 1, the process for establishing what is tight begins by building shared knowledge throughout the faculty regarding the current reality of the school and the most-promising practices for meeting the needs of students. When educators base their decisions on evidence of these promising practices, principals and teachers should be able to agree that the following stipulations are nondiscretionary.

- The behavior and practices of all staff must align with and support the shared vision and collective commitments that drive the work of the school.

- The fundamental structure of the school must be the collaborative team. Staff members may not work in isolation. They must contribute to the team process, honor team commitments, and work interdependently with their colleagues to achieve the team's SMART goal.

- Each team must establish a guaranteed and viable curriculum, unit by unit.

- Each team must monitor the learning of every student on an ongoing basis. This process for monitoring must include multiple team-developed common formative assessments.

- Each team must use the evidence of student learning that it gathers through its assessment process to inform and improve the instructional practice of individual members and to help the team identify and solve problems in student learning.

- Each team must use the evidence of student learning that it gathers through its assessment process to identify students who need intervention and enrichment.

- The school must establish a systematic process of intervention and enrichment that ensures students receive additional time and support for learning targeted to their individual needs.

Note that within these tight parameters educators are empowered to make very important decisions. Each team is empowered to play a crucial role in determining what students must learn, the pacing of the curriculum, the tools it will use to gather evidence of student learning, and the strategies it will use to address issues in student learning. Each team is empowered to establish its own collective commitments and its own SMART goals. Individual teachers are empowered to use the instructional strategies they feel are most effective in helping their students learn. This attention to empowering teachers within the PLC process represents the loose part of the school's culture, but no one has the autonomy to opt out of that process.

Communicating What Is Tight

Marcus Buckingham (2005) argues that the single most important thing leaders must remember is communicating clearly and consistently to people throughout the organization. The key to this clear communication is not eloquence. It is not what leaders say that helps people understand organizational priorities but rather what leaders do and the consistency—the redundancy—with which they do it.

The following communications audit adapted from DuFour and colleagues (2010) is designed to help principals assess the effectiveness of their communication. We recommend that the principal reflect on how he or she would respond to the following questions, and then invite staff members to respond to the same questions through surveys or small-group dialogues.

What systems have been put in place in our school to ensure that our articulated priorities are being addressed?

When something is truly a priority in an organization, people do not *hope* it happens; they develop and implement systematic plans to *ensure* that it happens.

- Do we have systems for clarifying what students must learn?

- Do we have systems for monitoring student learning?

- Do we have systems for responding when students have difficulty?

- Do we have systems for enriching and extending learning for students who are proficient?

- Do we have systems for monitoring and supporting teams?

- Do we have systems for providing each teacher and team with the timely information on student learning that is essential to continuous improvement?

What do we monitor in our school?

In most organizations, what gets monitored gets done. Effective schools establish the indicators of progress to be monitored, the process for monitoring them, and the means of sharing results with people throughout the school.

- How do we monitor student learning?

- How do we monitor the work and the effectiveness of our collaborative teams?

- How do we monitor the effectiveness of our system of intervention and enrichment?

- How do we monitor the progress our school is making on the PLC journey?

What questions do we ask in our school?

The questions that an organization poses and the effort and energy spent in the pursuit of those questions not only communicate priorities but also point members in a particular direction.

- What questions are we asking people to resolve through collective inquiry?

- What questions drive the work of individuals and teams throughout our organization?

- What questions drive the work of our faculty meetings?

How do we allocate resources (time, money, and people) in our school?

The decisions made regarding the expenditure of precious resources are some of the most unequivocal ways organizations communicate what is important.

- How do we provide time for our collaborative teams to engage in collective inquiry?

- How are teams using the time that has been provided?

- How do we provide time for intervention and enrichment for our students?

- Are we using our financial and human resources most effectively?

Do I model what I ask of others?

A summary of thirty years on effective leadership concludes, "You either lead by example or you don't lead at all" (Kouzes & Posner, 2010, p. xxiii). Another study of learning organizations concludes, "The single most powerful mechanism for creating a learning environment is that the leadership of the organization be willing to model the approach to learning they want others to embrace" (Thompson, 2006, p. 96).

- What evidence shows that I am committed to and focused on high levels of learning for all students?

- What evidence shows that I am committed to building a collaborative culture?

- Do I use evidence of student learning to inform and improve my own practice as principal?

- Have I maintained a focus on our articulated priorities and attempted to protect staff from initiatives that do not reflect those priorities?

What do we celebrate in our school?

When an organization makes a concerted effort to call attention to and celebrate progress toward its goals, examples of commitments being demonstrated in day-to-day work, and evidence of improved results, people within the organization are continually reminded of the priorities and what it takes to achieve them. We will address this aspect of the PLC culture more fully in chapter 9.

- What process is in place to help identify teams that are improving?

- How do we acknowledge and celebrate improvement?

- Do we celebrate the effort expended and the knowledge gained when our initiatives do not achieve the results we intended?

- Who are the heroes in our school?

What are we willing to confront in our school?

If a leadership team hopes to convey what is important and valued, it must be prepared to confront those who act in ways that are contrary to the priorities of the school and the commitments of the staff.

- Do I as principal confront those who ignore what we contend is tight in our school?

- Do I confront those who do not honor the collective commitments we have made as a school?

- Do we confront our colleagues who do not honor their collective commitments to their teammates?

Being a Leader Who Is Willing to Confront

A school can succeed in creating a culture that is simultaneously loose and tight only if its leaders are willing to confront behavior that clearly violates the school's articulated core principles and priorities. Leaders who hope to communicate effectively must align what they do with what they say. If they insist that something is tight or nondiscretionary, and then ignore those who refuse to operate within the specified parameters, they will lose all credibility with staff. As Robert Evans (2001) concludes, "confrontation forms a matching bookend with clarity and focus" (p. 288).

Imagine that you have a staff member who refuses to be a contributing member to his collaborative team. As principal, you recognize you must confront that staff member. Here are some recommendations to consider.

- **Focus on the behavior rather than the person:** Confronting inappropriate behavior is not the same as demeaning or vilifying an individual. Recognize that the resistant staff member probably has what he feels are valid and legitimate reasons for disregarding what is intended to be tight. You can disapprove of the behavior and yet honor the person.

- **Think of what you want to happen and what you don't want to happen as a result of confronting the staff member:** Reflect on the outcome you hope will result from the conversation as well as the outcomes you hope to avoid. For example, a principal might say, "I hope that as a result of this meeting the staff member will change his behavior and other staff members will recognize that I will hold them accountable to the collaborative team process. I don't want this teacher to feel that I object to him as a person or that I don't value his past contribution to the school. I don't want to vent about my frustrations with this teacher."

- **Prepare:** Preparation is the prerequisite homework for the dialogue you are about to have. Anticipate what the staff member will say. Mentally rehearse how you will respond. Gather evidence to support your position. Most importantly, alert the superintendent or the appropriate central office staff of what you intend to do prior to the conversation with the teacher. Make certain they are aware of the problem and that they will support your proposed course of action.

- **State specific concerns:** Present concrete examples of the behaviors that have caused you concern. Avoid ambiguity ("You don't seem to buy in to what we are doing") and generalizations ("You always have a negative impact at team meetings because you never contribute"). Be specific about the behavior that troubles you.

- **Invite a response:** Ask the staff member to respond to the concerns. Listen attentively. Seek to understand. ("Help me understand your concern about working with your colleagues. Can you think of ways that we can make the experience a positive one for you?")

- **Present your rationale for why he or she should engage in the behavior:** Howard Gardner (2004) offers seven strategies for changing someone's mind. Let's apply those strategies to a staff member who refuses to contribute to the collaborative team process.

  1. **Rationale thinking**—"Doesn't it make sense that people who work together interdependently in a collective effort can accomplish more than people who work in isolation? Why would the professional organizations that represent teachers call on them to work collaboratively if it was not in their best interests?"

  2. **Research**—"I have gathered some of the research on the benefits of working as a PLC in which teachers work with colleagues to establish a guaranteed curriculum, use frequent common assessments to monitor each student's learning, and help each other build on their instructional strengths and address their weaknesses. Do you have research that supports working in isolation? In light of the evidence, and in the virtual absence of contradictory research, don't we have a professional obligation to implement this process?"

  3. **Resonance**—"I know you entered this profession to make a difference in the lives of kids and that you have impacted many of your students in a positive way during your years here. This is a way for you to extend your influence outside of your classroom to impact even more students."

  4. **Representational redescription**—"You indicated that you feel your past results prove you do not need to work with other people to be effective. This process will actually give you an opportunity to share your most effective strategies with your colleagues. This isn't about addressing your deficiencies; it is about sharing your strengths."

  5. **Resources and rewards**—"You have been urging me to create a science fair. If you commit to become a positive contributing member of your team, I will commit to presenting the science fair proposal to the central office."

  6. **Real-world events**—"You have expressed concerns about the negative things you *think* will happen if we embrace the PLC process. I will take you on a field trip to a school that has been highly effective in implementing the PLC process, and you can see how it actually works."

  7. **Require**—If none of these first six arguments succeed in persuading the person to change his behavior, you must resort to this final strategy. In effect, you advise the staff member, "I understand that you would prefer not to do this, but I am directing you to do it. To be certain there is no misunderstanding, tomorrow I will present you with a written directive that outlines the very specific behaviors I expect to see from you and the evidence we will gather together to demonstrate you are doing what you have been directed to do. I will help you in any way I can to succeed in what I am

asking you to do; but if you do not act according to this directive, I will consider it insubordination."

From that point on, the principal must monitor the teacher's behavior, not his attitude. A principal cannot require a teacher to be happy about collaborating with colleagues, but a principal can require that a teacher will collaborate, honor norms, teach the guaranteed curriculum, administer the common assessments, and so on. We prefer the teacher to act out of commitment, not compliance. For many people, however, commitment follows a personal experience; it does not precede it. If, as a result of participating in the collaborative team process, the teacher finds that it is beneficial, he will become more positive about and more committed to the process.

What if the principal believes that some staff members are so oppositional there is very little likelihood of changing their behavior? Should the principal confront those individuals when the possibility of a positive outcome seems remote, and the likelihood of disciplinary action seems almost inevitable? The answer to that question is a resounding *yes!* The willingness of the principal to confront a resister not only sends a message to the individual staff member but also communicates priorities to people throughout the school. As Kerry Patterson et al. (2008) write,

> Lack of punishment sends a loud message across organizations. The point isn't that people need to be threatened to perform. The point is that if you are unwilling to go to the mat when people violate a core value (such as giving their best effort), that value loses its moral force in the organization. On the other hand, you send a powerful message about your values when you hold people accountable. (p. 216)

If the school has engaged in the process we outlined in chapter 1, and therefore has the benefit of *shared* mission, vision, collective commitments, and goals, it becomes even more important for principals to address inappropriate behavior. When the staff has clarified the school it hopes to create, the principal must demonstrate a willingness to promote and protect the staff's collective priorities. In this situation, the principal champions the aspirations and expectations of the faculty, not merely his or her individual values.

It is natural for principals to hope to be universally admired, if not loved, by the faculty. However, effective leaders "must be willing and able to be unloved and settle for less than universal affection" (Burns, 1982, p. 34). Principals must recognize that if they engage in school improvement efforts that disrupt some of the traditional elements of the structures and culture of their schools, not everyone will be happy. Conflict is an inevitable by-product of substantive change, and principals will be ineffective in leading a PLC if their top priority is keeping the peace and ensuring the happiness of adults. The culture of any school will be determined to a large extent by the worst behavior the principal is willing to tolerate, because it sends the message to the rest of the staff that the behavior is acceptable.

There are many responsibilities that principals can and should delegate. They need to empower others and to remove some managerial tasks from their plates in order to devote more time and attention to leading the PLC process. One thing principals cannot delegate, however, is the responsibility to be directive when some staff members ignore the school's tight purpose and parameters.

Only one person in a school has the authority to tell a teacher, "I am directing you to do this," and the principals must be willing to use that authority.

Giving the Gift of Coherence

When, over an extended period of time, a principal's words and actions clearly and unequivocally communicate the purpose, priorities, and nondiscretionary processes that will drive the work of the school, that principal provides staff with a rare gift often lacking in today's school—coherence. In too many schools, educators see little or no relationship between the waves of initiatives that flood over them. In too many instances, they receive mixed messages about priorities or are told, "Pay attention to everything—everything is a priority." A school without focus is a school that cannot improve student learning. Remember Richard Elmore's (2004) admonition, "Organizational coherence on basic aims and values, then, is a precondition for the exercise of any effective leadership around instructional improvement" (p. 63).

See "The Professional Learning Communities at Work™ Continuum: Effective Communication," "The Professional Learning Communities at Work™ Continuum: Responding to Conflict," "Where Do We Go From Here? Worksheet: Effective Communication (Chapter 2)," and "Where Do We Go From Here? Worksheet: Effective Communication (Chapter 9)" for information to guide your next steps on your PLC journey. Visit **go.solution-tree.com/plcbooks** to download these reproducibles.

Sustaining School Improvement

"This too shall pass" is a common mantra that U.S. teachers have about school improvement proposals. They have every reason to feel that way. Between 1987 and 1997, *Phi Delta Kappan* articles offered 361 different ideas for making U.S. schools more effective (Carpenter, 2000), and that number has dramatically increased in the decade since the passage of No Child Left Behind. Veteran teachers who have watched these initiatives come and go have become inured to the cyclical process of the rise and fall of improvement programs. A new program is announced with great fanfare and promise only to be met by confusion, concerns, and criticism. As complaints mount and immediate benefits fail to materialize, the initiative is abandoned, and the search begins for the next magic bullet.

Although educators are accustomed to *initiating* school improvement strategies, they have precious little experience in *sustaining* improvement initiatives. Principals have played a significant role in creating this cycle of short-lived reform efforts, and it will take effective leadership on the part of principals to break the cycle. In this chapter, we examine three keys to sustaining the meaningful improvement initiatives in your school.

1. Plan for short-term wins.

2. Persevere.

3. Build the capacity of people throughout the school to contribute to the leadership of the PLC process.

Plan for Short-Term Wins

Researchers from both inside and outside education have examined the question of how effective leaders help people maintain focus during their improvement efforts (Amabile & Kramer, 2010; Blanchard, 2007; Elmore & City, 2007; Fullan, 2011b; Kotter & Cohen, 2002; Patterson et al., 2008). They offer remarkably consistent advice: plan for short-term wins. We have emphasized throughout this book that the PLC process is a journey rather than an event. However, most people won't continue on that journey unless early on they see evidence that it is taking them where they want to go. The identification and celebration of short-term wins provide that evidence. As Jim Collins (2001) writes:

> When people see tangible results, however incremental at first, and see how the results flow from the overall concept, they will line up with enthusiasm. People want to be a part of a winning team. They want to contribute to producing visible, tangible results. They want to feel the excitement of being involved in something that works. When they feel the magic of momentum, when they can begin to see tangible results—that's when they get on board. (p. 178)

Planning for short-term wins is very different from hoping for short-term wins. Effective principals translate the complex PLC process into a series of incremental, doable steps and establish frequent benchmarks and milestones that help to build a sense of momentum and progress. They celebrate when every team has established collective commitments and SMART goals. They applaud a grade-level team for establishing its guaranteed curriculum and administering its first common assessment. They recognize a team that has identified and addressed a significant deficit in student learning because of the members' collective analysis of data from a common assessment. They tell stories of students who moved from failure to success because of the collective efforts of staff members engaged in the school's systematic interventions. They are vigilant in searching for evidence that students are learning at higher levels, they call attention to progress, and they seek every opportunity to express appreciation and admiration for the individual and collective efforts that are contributing to that progress. This attention to the celebration of short-term wins helps people throughout the organization believe in their collective ability "to solve the next problem *because they have done it so many times before*" (Fullan, 2011a, p. 108, emphasis in original).

The achievement of short-term wins will not, however, fuel the improvement process if people are unaware of them. Therefore, principals must not only plan for evidence of progress but must also plan to celebrate the progress in a very public way. As we mentioned in chapter 8, public celebration is a powerful way to communicate what is valued in a school.

See "Why Should Celebration Be a Part of Our Culture?" for a sampling of the research on celebration. Visit **go.solution-tree.com/plcbooks** to download this reproducible.

The idea that schools should make a concerted effort to recognize and celebrate the effort of individuals, teams, and faculty members runs counter to traditional practice. Some educators argue that we shouldn't acknowledge people for merely doing what they are paid to do. Others express concern that if some staff members or teams are cited, others might feel slighted, and they would prefer that no one be honored rather than risk offending someone. Still others argue that if celebration becomes a regular part of the school's practice, it will become commonplace and meaningless.

Yet study after study of what workers want in their jobs offers the same conclusions: they want to feel appreciated and that their efforts are making a positive difference. One of those studies found that the single best motivator for knowledge workers is celebration of progress. The authors advise leaders to set clear short-term goals, to proactively create the perception of progress, and to celebrate incremental progress (Amabile & Kramer, 2010).

The identification and celebration of small wins should be part of the routine practice of any school committed to continuing on the PLC journey. Although principals must help to create the conditions to support this public recognition in their schools, they should not be solely responsible for celebration. An interim step might be assigning this responsibility to the guiding coalition or to a special task force to oversee celebration. Ultimately, however, every individual in the school should be called on to contribute to the collective effort to recognize, appreciate, and applaud their colleagues who are making progress on the PLC journey.

Persevere

We have yet to encounter any school that implemented the PLC process and did not make mistakes, did not confront unforeseen obstacles, or did not encounter resistance. What separates the schools that succeed versus those who succumb is the willingness of the principal and staff to persist in the face of problems rather than retreat from them. If principals view these challenges as evidence that the process is without merit, that they lack the expertise to create a PLC, or that factors outside their sphere of influence prevent them from successful implementation, they abandon the process and retreat to the comfort of the familiar status quo.

Rather than flit from initiative to initiative, effective principals push in a constant direction over an extended period of time and maintain a laser-like focus on the few key factors that have the greatest impact on student learning. Fullan (2011a) refers to this as *resolute leadership* and contends that staying the course is a characteristic of all organizations that are successful over the long term.

In reflecting on his own experience as a school principal, the director of the Center for Comprehensive School Reform and Improvement offers this advice to principals:

> In hindsight, I see that moving forward and doing something innovative often won out over painstakingly measuring our progress and adjusting our strategies. My advice? Stay the course. Work the plan. Monitor progress and analyze results. It's not glamorous; it doesn't make headlines. But patience and persistence work when trying to achieve success at this most difficult of tasks—improving a school. (Burkett, 2006, p. 3)

Principals who demonstrate the tenacity and willingness to persist in the face of obstacles are typically driven by a moral imperative. One of the most comprehensive studies of district and school leadership that has ever been conducted found that the most effective principals consider their position as a *calling* rather than a *job*. They were driven to make a positive difference in the lives of their students, and this drive helps them to sustain their effort during troubled times (Louis et al., 2010).

Build the Leadership Capacity of People Throughout the School

If widely distributed leadership is vital to implementing the PLC process, as we argued in chapter 1, it is even more important in sustaining that process. Educators have mistakenly come to believe that changes of leadership will inevitably result in changes of direction. This perception is valid if the previous principal was the sole or even the primary champion of that process. If, however, that principal has delegated authority, created collaborative decision-making processes, led from the center rather than the top, and purposefully built the capacity of people throughout the school to serve as leaders, the improvement process will have many champions rather than one. In this school culture, changes in the principalship do not automatically result in changes in direction, because there are many leaders prepared to continue the work. As one study of PLCs concludes, "The message is unequivocal: sustaining the impact of improvement requires the leadership capability of many rather than a few" (Bezzina, 2006, p. 164).

We both had the privilege of serving as principals of high-performing PLCs that received state and national recognition for their effectiveness in helping students learn at high levels. When we left our respective positions, the faculties of both schools petitioned the superintendent to ensure that the new principal was totally committed to continuing their PLC process. Since that time, Rick's former school has had five different principals, and Becky's has had four; however, in both instances, the schools have continued on the PLC journey and have steadily improved student achievement beyond the levels when we were the principals.

The real test of a principal's leadership will not be limited to how well students achieve during his or her tenure. The ultimate test will be how many leaders that principal has left behind who are capable of and committed to continuing the school improvement journey. Ironically, your skill as a leader will not be fully revealed until you are no longer leading.

10

Fostering Collective Efficacy

We began this book asking readers to consider an important question, What is the role of the principal? We have argued that the primary responsibility of the principal is to lead a collective effort to create a professional learning community that ensures high levels of learning for students through recursive processes that promote adult learning. We have attempted to offer specific, practical, and actionable steps principals can take to fulfill that role.

We conclude with another question, Do you believe in your ability to fulfill this role and the collective ability of your staff to create such a school? In essence, we are asking, "Do you believe you can make a difference?" The answer to this question will have an enormous impact on your effectiveness as a principal. As Kouzes and Posner (2010) write,

> Everything you will ever do as a leader is based on one audacious assumption. It's the assumption that *you matter*. Before you can lead others, you have to lead yourself and believe that you can have a positive impact on others. You have to believe that your words can inspire and your actions can move others. You have to believe that what you do counts for something. If you don't, you won't even try. Leadership begins with you. The Truth Is That You Make a Difference. (p. 1)

Principals who believe in their ability to make a difference focus on factors within their sphere of influence rather than assigning blame to external factors beyond their locus of control. They approach challenges with optimism, confident that those challenges ultimately can be overcome through their personal efforts and the collective efforts of the staff. It is not the absence of problems that defines effective principals but rather their willingness to learn from the problems, believe they will succeed, and tenaciously stay the course rather than retreat.

The link between the principal's sense of efficacy and student achievement has been established in two comprehensive studies of school leadership (Louis et al., 2010; Reeves, 2011). To assess a principal's sense of efficacy, Louis and colleagues (2010) ask the following questions. Consider how you would respond to each.

To what extent do you feel you are able to:

- Motivate teachers?

- Generate enthusiasm for the school's shared vision?

- Manage change in your school?

- Create a positive learning environment in your school?

- Facilitate student learning in your school?

- Raise achievement on standardized tests?

Collective Efficacy

Effective principals not only believe in their own ability to make a difference but also help others throughout the school to believe in their individual and collective capacity to impact student achievement. Once again the link between staff members' belief in their ability to help students learn and high levels of student achievement is well established in research. In fact, the collective efficacy of staff is a better predictor of their students' success than the socioeconomic status of the students (Goddard, Hoy, & Hoy, 2004).

So, how do principals promote a sense of collective efficacy throughout a school? The strategies we have presented throughout this book provide a blueprint. Teachers are more likely to believe in their ability to make a difference when:

- They have a shared vision of the school they are trying to create, the specific commitments they must honor to create such a school, and targets and timelines that help them mark their progress

- They are clear on what they want students to learn and how students will demonstrate that learning

- They are working as part of a collaborative, collective effort to meet the needs of students rather than in isolation

- The collaborative process calls on teams to establish SMART goals and pursue them until they are achieved

- A process is in place to provide teachers with irrefutable evidence that students are achieving at higher levels

- The school has a process to provide students with systematic intervention and enrichment

- The improvement process is divided into small, incremental steps that create short-term wins that are publicly celebrated

- The principal models his or her conviction that the staff have the knowledge and skills to help all students learn

As principal, your beliefs and emotions are important because they are contagious (Goleman et al., 2002). If you are determined to impact the lives of your students, if you believe that it lies within your sphere of influence to do so, and if you are willing to pursue that goal with fierce resolve despite the problems you encounter, you will likely influence your faculty to do the same.

To assess the collective efficacy of your staff members, survey them or engage them in small-group dialogue to determine their level of agreement with the following statements (Louis et al., 2010).

To what extent do you agree that:

- The staff members of our school have the knowledge and skills they need to improve student learning

- Most of our staff view continuous improvement as a necessary part of every job

- We view problems in this school as issues to be solved, not as barriers to action

- Our staff members communicate a belief in the capacity of teachers to teach even the most difficult students

If it becomes apparent that many staff members are convinced there is little they can do to impact student achievement, remember Howard Gardner's (2004) advice to present them with real-world evidence that runs counter to their beliefs. One important way to help foster collective efficacy is to demonstrate that there are schools similar to your own that have been highly successful in implementing the PLC process in ways that have had a dramatic impact on student learning. All Things PLC (www.allthingsplc.info) is a great tool for demonstrating that real schools facing real challenges are making a real difference for their students.

Are you in an urban setting with high-poverty and a high-minority population? Look at the results from Mount Eagle Elementary in Alexandria, Virginia; Highland Elementary in Montgomery County, Maryland; Stults Road Elementary in Dallas, Texas; or Mark Twain Middle in Fairfax County, Virginia. Are you in a high-poverty rural setting? The Sanger School District in California has the lowest-per capita income among the 435 congressional districts in the United States, yet has demonstrated dramatic gains in student achievement since embracing the PLC process in 2006. Are you in a very small school? Consider Pennfield Elementary in New Brunswick, Canada, with 63 students; Henry Elementary in Henry, Virginia, with 200 students; or Yuma Middle School in Yuma, Colorado, with 238 students. Conversely, Wyndham Lakes Elementary in Orlando, Florida; Liberty Junior High School in Liberty, Missouri; and Lakeridge Junior High in Orem, Utah, have demonstrated that schools with over 1,000 students can excel at the PLC process. (In fact, there are highly successful high schools featured on All Things PLC with over 3,000 students.) Are you a school that seems stuck with little improvement over time? So was Schaumburg Elementary District 54, the largest elementary school district in Illinois, that has moved from the middle of the state's ranking in student achievement to become one of the top 10 percent of districts in Illinois. Are you concerned about how to persuade educators in a *good school* in which students are already performing at high levels that they can continue to raise achievement year after year? Study the elementary and middle schools in Kildeer Countryside District 96 in Buffalo Grove, Illinois, all of which made the leap from *good* to *great*.

Peruse the "Evidence of Effectiveness" portion of the All Things PLC website (www.allthingsplc .info/evidence/evidence.php) to find hundreds of schools that have raised student achievement by implementing the PLC at Work process. Perhaps you can take staff on a field trip to visit one of the model PLC schools or arrange for a video conference that will allow your teachers to ask questions of teachers who have experienced the benefits of working in a school that operates as a PLC. Helping your staff members recognize and embrace their collective efficacy is one of the greatest gifts you can give them.

Conclusion

In a very real sense, this entire book has been devoted to answering the question that began it, What is the role of the principal? We have attempted to go beyond the accurate but generic admonition, "to lead a professional learning community," by offering specific responsibilities you must address in order to create such a school. Once again these responsibilities include the following:

- Clarify the purpose, vision, collective commitments, and goals that define your school.

- Create a culture that is simultaneously loose and tight, and clearly communicate the purpose and priorities of your school.

- Use the collaborative team as the fundamental structure of your school, and put systems in place to facilitate and support the collaborative team process.

- Ensure that students have access to a guaranteed and viable curriculum.

- Monitor each student's learning through an ongoing assessment process that includes multiple team-developed common formative assessments.

- Provide every teacher and every team with access to ongoing evidence of student learning, and ensure they use that evidence to inform and improve their individual and collective practice.

- Provide students who struggle with additional time and support for learning in a way that is timely, directive, precise, and systematic, and provide students who are proficient with opportunities for enrichment.

- Demonstrate reciprocal accountability by providing staff members with the time, resources, and support that enable them to succeed at what you are asking them to do.

- Persevere in the face of obstacles and setbacks, and never lose faith that your efforts and the collective efforts of the staff can overcome those challenges and ultimately lead to higher levels of student achievement.

- Stay the course.

- Disperse leadership throughout the school, and build such a strong collaborative culture that those other leaders can continue the PLC journey long after you have left the school.

This is the role of the principal, a role that is daunting, but doable.

If you serve in the principalship in the coming year, you can be certain that you will work hard. What is not certain is if you will focus on the right work. Your ability to define what constitutes the right work and to focus the collective effort of the staff on that work will determine the effectiveness of your school. You are in the pivotal role. Don't ask, "Will I make a difference?" You will. The only question left for you to answer is, "What difference will I make?" We hope that this book and the others that will follow it in the *Essentials for Principals* series help you to provide the leadership that will make a positive difference in the lives of the students and staff you were hired to serve.

REFERENCES

Amabile, T. M., & Kramer, S. J. (2010). What really motivates workers: Understanding the power of progress. *Harvard Business Review, 88*(1), 44–45.

Barber, M., & Mourshed, M. (2007). *How the world's best-performing school systems come out on top.* New York: McKinsey. Accessed at www.mckinsey.com/App_Media/Reports/SSO/Worlds_School_Systems_Final.pdf on January 1, 2010.

Barber, M., & Mourshed, M. (2009). *Shaping the future: How good education systems can become great in the decade ahead—Report on the International Education Roundtable—7 July 2009, Singapore.* Accessed at www.mckinsey.com/locations/southeastasia/knowledge/Education_Roundtable.pdf on January 1, 2011.

Bennis, W. (2000). *Managing the dream: Reflections on leadership and change.* Cambridge, MA: Perseus.

Bezzina, C. (2006). The road less traveled: Professional learning communities in secondary schools. *Theory Into Practice, 45*(2), 159–167.

Black, P., Harrison, C., Lee, C., Marshall, B., & Wiliam, D. (2004). Working inside the black box: Assessment for learning in the classroom. *Phi Delta Kappan, 86*(1), 9–19.

Blanchard, K. (2007). *Leading at a higher level: Blanchard on leadership and creating high-performing organizations.* New York: Prentice Hall.

Bloom, B. (1980). *All our children learning.* New York: McGraw-Hill.

Buckingham, M. (2005). *The one thing you need to know: About great managing, great leading, and sustained individual success.* New York: Free Press.

Buffum, A., Mattos, M., & Weber, C. (2009). *Pyramid response to intervention: RTI, Professional Learning Communities, and How to Respond When Kids Don't Learn.* Bloomington, IN: Solution Tree Press.

Burkett, H. (2006). *Six don'ts of school improvement . . . and their solutions.* Washington, DC: Center for Comprehensive School Reform and Improvement.

Burns, J. M. (1982). *Leadership.* New York: Harper & Row.

Carpenter, W. A. (2000). Ten years of silver bullets: Dissenting thoughts on education reform. *Phi Delta Kappan, 81*(5), 383–389.

Collins, J. (2001). *Good to great: Why some companies make the leap—and others don't.* New York: HarperBusiness.

Collins, J. C., & Porras, J. I. (1997). *Built to last: Successful habits of visionary companies.* New York: HarperBusiness.

Covey, S. (1989). *The seven habits of highly effective people: Powerful lessons in personal change.* New York: Fireside.

Duffett, A., Farkas, S., Rotherham, A. J., & Silva, E. (2008). *Waiting to be won over: Teachers speak on the profession, unions, and reform.* Washington, DC: Education Sector.

DuFour, R., DuFour, R., Eaker, R., & Many, T. (2010). *Learning by doing: A handbook for professional learning communities at work* (2nd ed.). Bloomington, IN: Solution Tree Press.

DuFour, R., & Marzano, R. J. (2011). *Leaders of learning: How district, school, and classroom leaders improve student achievement.* Bloomington, IN: Solution Tree Press.

Elmore, R. F. (2004). *School reform from the inside out: Policy, practice, and performance.* Cambridge, MA: Harvard Education Press.

Elmore, R., & City, E. (2007). The road to school improvement. *Harvard Education Newsletter, 23*(3). Accessed at www.hepg.org/hel/article/229 on January 1, 2011.

Evans, R. (2001). *The human side of school change: Reform, resistance and the real-life problems of innovation.* San Francisco: Jossey-Bass.

Fullan, M. (2010). *All systems go: The change imperative for whole system reform.* Thousand Oaks, CA: Corwin Press.

Fullan, M. (2011a). *Change leader: Learning to do what matters most.* San Francisco: Jossey-Bass.

Fullan, M. (2011b). *The moral imperative realized.* Thousand Oaks, CA: Corwin Press.

Gallimore, R., Ermeling, B., Saunders, W., & Goldenberg, C. (2009). Moving the learing of teaching closer to practice: Teacher education implications of school-based inquiry teams. *The Elementary School Journal, 109*(5), 537–551.

Gardner, H. (2004). *Changing minds: The art and science of changing our own and other people's minds.* Boston: Harvard Business School Press.

Goddard, R. D., Hoy, W. K., & Hoy, A. W. (2004). Collective efficacy beliefs: Theoretical developments, empirical evidence, and future directions. *Educational Researcher, 33*(3), 3–13.

Goleman, D., Boyatzis, R., & McKee, A. (2002). *Primal leadership: Learning to lead with emotional intelligence.* Boston: Harvard Business School Press.

Guskey, T. (1996). *Implementing mastery learning.* Independence, KY: Wadsworth.

Hattie, J. A. C. (2009). *Visible learning: A synthesis of over 800 meta-analyses relating to achievement.* New York: Routledge.

Johnson, S. M., & Kardos, S. M. (2007). Professional culture and the promise of colleagues. In S. M. Johnson & the Project on the Next Generation of Teachers, *Finders and keepers: Helping new teachers survive and thrive in our schools* (pp. 139–166). San Francisco: Jossey-Bass.

Katzenbach, J. R., & Smith, D. K. (2003). *The wisdom of teams: Creating the high-performance organization.* New York: HarperBusiness.

Kotter, J. P., & Cohen, D. S. (2002). *The heart of change. Real-life stories of how people change their organizations.* Boston: Harvard Business School Press.

Kouzes, J. M., & Posner, B. Z. (2010). *The truth about leadership: The no-fads, heart-of-the-matter facts you need to know.* San Francisco: Jossey-Bass.

Learning Forward. (2011). *Standards for professional learning.* Accessed at www.learningforward.org /standards/learningcommunities/index.cfm on September 11, 2011.

Leithwood, K., Louis, K. S., Anderson, S., & Wahlstrom, K. (2004). *How leadership influences student learning.* Minneapolis. MN: Center for Applied Research and Educational Improvement.

Lezotte, L. (1991). *Correlates of effective schools: The first and second generation.* Okemos, MI: Effective Schools Products.

Little, J. W. (2006). *Professional community and professional development in the learning-centered school.* Washington, DC: National Education Association.

Little, J. W., & Bartlett, L. (2010). The teacher workforce and problems of educational equity. *Review of Research in Education, 34*(1), 285–328.

Louis, K. S., Leithwood, K., Wahlstrom, K. L., & Anderson, S. E. (2010). *Learning from leadership: Investigating the links to improved student learning.* Minneapolis, MN: Center for Applied Research and Educational Improvement.

Marzano, R. J. (2003). *What works in schools: Translating research into action.* Alexandria, VA: Association for Supervision and Curriculum Development.

Marzano, R. J. (2009). Setting the record straight on "high-yield" strategies. *Phi Delta Kappan, 91*(1), 30–37.

Marzano, R. J., Waters, T., & McNulty, B. A. (2005). *School leadership that works: From research to results.* Alexandria, VA: Association for Supervision and Curriculum Development.

McLaughlin, M., & Talbot, J. (2006). *Building school-based teacher learning communities: Professional strategies to improve student achievement.* New York: Teachers College Press.

MetLife. (2010). *The MetLife survey of the American teacher: Collaborating for student success.* Accessed at www.metlife.com/about/corporate-profile/citizenship/metlife-foundation/metlife-survey-of-the -american-teacher.html?WT.mc_id=vu1101 on January 10, 2010.

Mourshed, M., Chijioke, C., & Barber, M. (2010). *How the world's most improved school systems keep getting better.* New York: McKinsey. Accessed at http://ssomckinsey.darbyfilms.com/reports /EducationBook_A4%20SINGLES_DEC%202.pdf on December 20, 2010.

National Association of Elementary School Principals. (2001). *Leading learning communities: Standards for what principals should know and be able to do.* Alexandria, VA: Author.

O'Neill, J., & Conzemius, A. (2006). *The power of SMART goals: Using goals to improve student learning.* Bloomington, IN: Solution Tree Press.

Patterson, K., Grenny, J., Maxfield, D., McMillan, R., & Switzler, A. (2008). *Influencer: The power to change anything.* New York: McGraw-Hill.

Pfeffer, J., & Sutton, R. (2000). *The knowing-doing gap: How smart companies turn knowledge into action.* Boston: Harvard Business School Press.

Popham, W. J. (2008). *Transformative assessment.* Alexandria, VA: Association for Supervision and Curriculum Development.

Popham, W. J. (2009). Curriculum mistakes to avoid. *American School Board Journal, 196*(11), 36–38.

Rebora, A. (2010). Interview: Responding to RTI. *Education Week Teacher PD Sourcebook, 3*(2), 20. Accessed at www.edweek.org/tsb/articles/2010/04/12/02allington.h03.html on July 26, 2011.

Reeves, D. B. (2002). *The leader's guide to standards: A blueprint for educational equity and excellence.* San Francisco: Jossey-Bass.

Reeves, D. B. (2004). *Accountability for learning: How teachers and school leaders can take charge.* Alexandria, VA: Association for Supervision and Curriculum Development.

Reeves, D. B. (2011). *Finding your leadership focus: What matters most for student results.* New York: Teachers College Press.

Robinson, M. A., Passantino, C., Acerra, M., Bae, L., Thiehen, K., Pido, E., et al. (2010). *School perspectives on collaborative inquiry: Lessons learned from New York City, 2009–2010.* New York: Consortium for Policy Research in Education.

Schaffer, R., & Thomson, H. (1998). Successful change programs begin with results. In *Harvard Business Review on Change* (pp. 189–214). Boston: Harvard Business School Press.

Sparks, D. (2004). Broader purpose calls for higher understanding: An interview with Andy Hargreaves. *Journal of Staff Development, 25*(2), 46–50.

Stiggins, R., & DuFour, R. (2009). Maximizing the power of formative assessments. *Phi Delta Kappan, 90*(9), 640–644.

Stigler, J., & Hiebert, J. (2009). Closing the teaching gap. *Phi Delta Kappan, 91*(3), 32–35.

Thompson, J. W. (2006). The renaissance of learning in business. In S. Chawla & J. Renesch (Eds.), *Learning organizations: Developing cultures for tomorrow's workplace* (pp. 85–100). New York: Productivity Press.

Weisberg, D., Sexton, S., Mulhern, J., & Keeling, D. (2009). *The widget effect: Our national failure to recognize differences in teacher effectiveness* (2nd ed.). Brooklyn, NY: The New Teacher Project. Accessed at http://widgeteffect.org/downloads/thewidgeteffect_execsummary.pdf on January 10, 2010.

INDEX

Effective Program Evaluation
Mardale Dunsworth and Dawn Billings
Educators are increasingly coming to realize the importance of making decisions based on reliable, accurate data. This short guide provides a blueprint for evaluating academic programs, practices, or strategies within a simple, effective framework. It includes a step-by-step walkthrough of the program evaluation cycle and an appendix that explains vital concepts and vocabulary in accessible language.
BKF461

Mobile Learning Devices
Kipp D. Rogers
This brief guide explains why mobile learning is transforming education and how devices such as cell phones can enhance learning in 21st century classrooms. The author provides guidelines principals can use to help staff introduce mobile learning devices into instruction in ways that are safe, engaging, aligned with National Educational Technology Standards, and targeted to promote student learning.
BKF445

Communicating & Connecting With Social Media
William M. Ferriter, Jason T. Ramsden, and Eric C. Sheninger
Social media holds great potential benefits for schools reaching out to our communities, preparing our teachers, and connecting with our kids. In this short text, the authors examine how enterprising schools are using social media tools to provide customized professional development for teachers and to transform communication practices with staff, students, parents, and other stakeholders.
BKF474

Learning by Doing
A Handbook for Professional Learning Communities at Work™
Richard DuFour, Rebecca DuFour, Robert Eaker, and Thomas Many
The second edition of *Learning by Doing* is an action guide for closing the knowing-doing gap and transforming schools into PLCs. It also includes seven major additions that equip educators with essential tools for confronting challenges.
BKF416

Leaders of Learning
How District, School, and Classroom Leaders Improve Student Achievement
Richard DuFour and Robert J. Marzano
For many years, the authors have been fellow travelers on the journey to help educators improve their schools. Their first coauthored book focuses on district leadership, principal leadership, and team leadership, and addresses how individual teachers can be most effective in leading students—by learning with colleagues how to implement the most promising pedagogy in their classrooms.
BKF455

Solution Tree | Press   Visit solution-tree.com or call 800.733.6786 to order.

Solution Tree

Solution Tree's mission is to advance the work of our authors. By working with the best researchers and educators worldwide, we strive to be the premier provider of innovative publishing, in-demand events, and inspired professional development designed to transform education to ensure that all students learn.

The mission of the National Association of Elementary School Principals is to lead in the advocacy and support for elementary and middle level principals and other education leaders in their commitment for all children.